Africa
A Beginner's Guide

D1009466

ONEWORLD BEGINNER'S GUIDES combine an original, inventive, and engaging approach with expert analysis on subjects ranging from art and history to religion and politics, and everything in between. Innovative and affordable, books in the series are perfect for anyone curious about the way the world works and the big ideas of our time.

Beginners
GUIDES

Africa
A Beginner's Guide

Tom Young

ONEWORLD
OXFORD

A Oneworld Book/Paperback Original

Published by Oneworld Publications 2010

Copyright © Tom Young 2010

ISBN 978–1–85168–753–4

Typeset by Jayvee, Trivandrum, India
Cover design by vaguelymemorable.com
Printed and bound by CPI Cox & Wyman, Reading, Berks, RG1 8EX

Oneworld Publications
UK: 185 Banbury Road, Oxford, OX2 7AR, England
USA: 38 Greene Street, 4th Floor, New York, NY 10013, USA

Learn more about Oneworld. Join our mailing list to
find out about our latest titles and special offers at:

www.oneworld-publications.com

Contents

Illustrations

Map 1 Independent Africa (image © David Berger)

Introduction: making sense of Africa

In recent years interest in Africa has surged: the outside world pours huge amounts of aid into the continent; international statesmen regularly discuss African issues; an enormous number of charities are involved in a limitless array of activities in African countries; many people have become involved in campaigns about debt and poverty; many more attended concerts about Nelson Mandela. Most remarkable of all, prominent political figures and celebrities have made statements to a wider public about Africa, as in Tony Blair's famous remark to a Labour Party conference that Africa is a 'scar on the conscience of mankind'. This interest and concern has generated a vast amount of material of all kinds, written and visual. That prompts the question: why another book on Africa and what is special about this one?

Writing this book has been shaped by two considerations. The first is to provide the interested reader with a guide to the sheer bulk of information and discussion that appears about Africa. As with any subject, circumstances change and often require us to revisit established understandings. It becomes necessary both to take account of new developments and to see them in the context of the past. To make the book manageable, its main focus is on politics, international relations, and what is now called 'development'. While concentrating on these aspects I have not hesitated to explain wider global changes or indeed historical experiences in other parts of the world where I thought they illuminated the African situation. As a result, aside from the occasional remark, there is nothing in here about African art or music or food, fascinating though all these are. I should also add that this book is about sub-Saharan Africa, so it excludes the countries of North Africa. There are those who argue that this is an unjustified separation, but it is conventional in much academic and other writing about Africa and I have followed that convention.

The second, and rather more important consideration, is to provide the general reader with some critical distance from much of the debate about Africa which is often both strident and partisan, and designed to convince, to establish a certain point of view, as much as to inform or analyse. We are all assailed by appeals from charities (and celebrities) to help 'end poverty' or 'prevent conflict' in Africa. The promoters of such appeals may be knowledgeable and well intentioned (they often are) but their primary purpose is to get us to see the world their way so that we then contribute to their cause – and in itself there is, of course, nothing wrong with this. You might be forgiven for thinking this is a rather modest aim. We all know that such causes are openly partisan and there are alternative sources of information and analysis that we can turn to, notably those provided by journalists and academics. It is true that journalists and academics are not so closely identified with 'causes', especially their rather less savoury practices of massaging facts and images to solicit money, but this does not mean that they do not have particular standpoints which may obscure certain realities, even if they dress these up in more sophisticated language.

The fact is that African studies, even in its more analytical and academic form, is often suffused by a certain kind of 'political correctness'. It claims to treat Africans with respect and yet in fact treats them as special cases, as objects of primarily moral concern; this is, in a way, to treat them like children. This is a rather bold assertion so let me give as an illustration something we will encounter again in this book – the issue of slavery, and especially the slave trade. Perhaps more than any other phenom-enon this one excites a peculiar horror in the Western mind and there is a vast literature that minutely examines and reports these horrors. Let me be clear: the point is not that this literature reports falsehoods; the point is rather that it emphasises some things and downplays others. One unpalatable fact is that while the trans-Atlantic trade was organised by Europeans, the slave trade within Africa itself was not. It was organised by Africans. It was precisely because Europeans had penetrated less far into Africa and knew less about it than any other part of the world (until well into the nineteenth century), that they were forced to rely on African middlemen and traders for their supply of slaves. Now of course perspectives get criticised and facts cannot be ignored indefinitely. The point I have just made is to be found in the academic literature, but it is rather obscured by the obsession with the moral wickedness of the trade itself.

There is a second rather less intellectual aspect to this. The slave trade is not just an obscure historians' squabble but something which is a politically contentious issue right now, because various pressure groups have made claims for compen-sation for slavery. For these claims to be plausible slavery has to be an exclusively European or Western evil. But the fact of African involvement in the slave trade requires us to be at least very careful about questions of moral responsibility, especially if we want to raise such questions as blame and compensation (we may, for example, conclude that it is not very fruitful to raise such issues about distant historical events). I might add that while writing this book the Civil Rights Congress of Nigeria was calling on traditional rulers in Africa to apologise for their ancestors' role in the trade.[1] We may conclude that we do want to raise issues of blame and compensation. But before we come to such conclusions we should be as clear as we can about what moral and political agendas are in play, and we should at least examine the facts as carefully as we can and without making too many prejudgements about them and, especially, without ignoring what African people themselves said and say about their own practices and beliefs.

That at least is the spirit in which I have written this short book about a very large place occupied by a very large number of people. You will not find in here the latest news about Africa; nor will you find heart-rending stories of human suffering to make you reach for your wallet; there are no searing indictments of colonial rulers or Africans who circumcise their female children to make you angry; nor, finally, are there any policy prescriptions about what must be done. What there is, I hope, is a sober assessment of the realities and some suggestions as to how it might be useful to think about them. The rest is up to you.

1

Africa before colonialism

This is not an historical book, but we usually find in human affairs that it is difficult to make sense of things until we have some idea of how they have developed over time. History is always controversial, not just because of the limitations of the material historians can find, but often because people's sense of themselves is bound up with their understanding of their history. A Scottish nationalist's view of Scotland's history will be rather different from an Englishman's, for example. When we turn to Africa further difficulties become apparent, two in particular. One of these is to do with the relative absence of written scripts, and therefore documents, from the continent, which means that much African history even today, despite all sorts of ingenious technical innovations devised by historians, remains rather speculative and controversial. A second concerns how we understand the notion of 'history' at all – and this is very contro- versial indeed. This issue turns on an idea that is deep seated in Western thought, namely the idea that some peoples are 'without history'. Famously articulated by the great German philosopher Hegel (for whom Africa was the 'land of child- hood'), its most notorious expression in recent times was by an eminent Oxford historian Hugh Trevor-Roper who remarked that there was no history in Africa but only 'the unedifying gyrations of barbarous tribes in picturesque but irrelevant corners of the globe'. It is customary to condemn such notions as 'racist' but (as so often) this accusation is shrill rather than illuminating. Here in any case it misses the point. This view of history was neither racist in any useful sense, nor indeed 'right-wing', since it was shared by that great revolutionary Karl Marx who praised British imperialism in India precisely because it would introduce elements of progress into Indian society.

That history writing is often linked to political agendas is very clear in the case of Africa. Almost as if in reaction to Trevor-Roper's remarks there was an explosion of historical writing about Africa from the 1960s onwards linked to the independence of African states, which now seemed to need their 'own' history, not that of the colonisers. Much of this historical writing, despite having remarks like Trevor-Roper's as its target, in fact shared many of his assumptions. History was about progress and the point was to prove that Africans were also part of that history, that they too had empires, cities, technology, and cultures; all the things thought to denote 'progress'. While among academic historians this kind of history has been replaced by something a little more objective, it still retains its grip – especially on more popular writing about Africa, much of which is not very subtly concerned to argue that Africans are 'just as good' as anyone else. These considerations are sometimes taken to mean that any attempt at historical understanding is a waste of time, as there is nothing but opinions. There are two reasons why this is a mistake. One is that new evidence comes to light that can enlarge our understanding. Such evidence may be better explained by one standpoint rather than another. But standpoints themselves can also be analysed and debated. So although we can understand how, and even why, debates about African history have become so emotionally charged, we can, I think, distance ourselves from them. A brief comparison may make the point. If historians of Japan are correct, the country was relatively technologically backward until recent times so, for example, just as in Africa, wheeled transport was not used much.

Nobody thinks that Japan or the Japanese are technologically 'backward' now, so these aspects of the Japanese past can be explained in ways that take account of history and geography, and indeed culture, without making demeaning or offensive inferences about particular peoples. It is, finally, important to be clear about our standpoints. The view taken in this book is firstly, that there are no significant biological differences between peoples that have any bearing on their historical development; and secondly, that there are important cultural differences about which we can learn but about which we should never, if at all, rush to judgement.

Environments

Controversies do not end with history – they rage in geography as well, though they are perhaps not so vehement. But it is worth noting that there has been a tendency in much recent social science and public discussion to play down the significance of geographical facts because they appear to induce a kind of fatalism or resignation which many people find objectionable. This attitude is deeply rooted in Western culture, which has long seen 'nature' as something to be controlled and dominated. It is reinforced by the fact that we live in an age of enormous advances both in scientific knowledge and in its application in the form of ever more effective technologies. In the face of such triumphs to stress the recalcitrance of nature seems almost a betrayal of humanity. But although all human societies grapple with the problems of social relations they also have to forge a relationship with the natural world, and this is always constrained by circumstances and environments. Even today in the West we are having to consider whether we can ignore our environment as much we have got used to since the late nineteenth century.

To follow a path through all these controversies I am going to limit myself to a set of observations about pre-colonial Africa which I think most scholars accept are plausible and which I also think go some way towards explaining more recent developments in the continent. This requires much generalisation about very big issues and there will always be exceptions to such generalisations, but the effort still seems worthwhile. It is worth making clear at the very outset what an enormous place we are dealing with. The continent of Africa is larger in size than the USA, Western Europe, and the Indian sub-continent put together. The figures are provided in Table 1 but the map below makes it clearer.

Table 1 Relative sizes of the continents

Asia	44,579,000 sq km
Africa	30,065,000 sq km
North America	24,256,000 sq km
South America	17,819,000 sq km
Europe	9,938,000 sq km

The sheer size of Africa alone has had important consequences for human activity, but there are many other features of this immense land mass that have had a considerable impact on the organisation of human communities. There is no doubt that, like other parts of the world, Africa is extremely physically diverse, containing a wide range of physical features and habitats, many of which are conducive to human settlement. But it is also true that in several ways it is quite a hostile environment for humans. Much of it is desert and semi-desert (the Sahara is the largest desert in the world and in area equals the United States including Alaska). It is one of the driest land masses on the globe with marked variations in rainfall, variations which are much higher in Africa than tropical Asia or America. It is not so much the total quantity of rainfall that is important as its distribution.

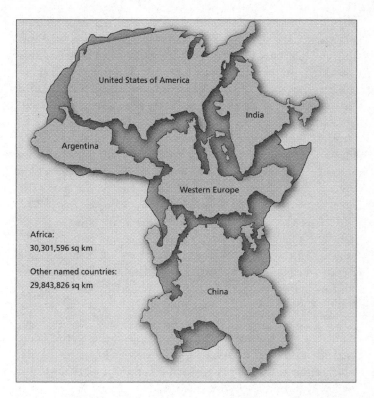

United States of America

India

Argentina

Western Europe

Africa:
30,301,596 sq km

Other named countries:
29,843,826 sq km

China

Map 2 Africa compared to other continents (image © David Berger)

Most of the African continent has wet and dry seasons rather than the four seasons characteristic of the earth's more temperate zones. Rainfall patterns are cyclical and rains can and do sometimes fail completely. Rates of evaporation are high and so a given amount of rainfall is less effective than in cooler parts of the world. Aside from its effects on what can be grown and when, the climate encourages a wide range of human and animal parasites which have sapped human vitality and restricted certain kinds of agricultural production. There is no winter in the tropics so insects and parasites flourish. Fatal endemic diseases include malaria, river blindness, sleeping sickness (trypanosomiasis), and bilharzia. The forms of malaria prevalent in Africa have been the more virulent ones which are often fatal, especially in children. Doctors in early colonial times estimated malaria killed 20% of young children in the Lake Nyasa region (modern Malawi). It is true that Africans have developed resistance to many of these pathogens, nevertheless many of them induce chronic conditions that are very debilitating. A number of other diseases, including dysentery, worms infestations, yaws, and leprosy, although rarely fatal, also drain vitality and lower life expectancy. A recent scientific paper suggests that, 'The neglected tropical diseases (NTDs) are the most common conditions affecting the poorest 500 million people living in sub-Saharan Africa (SSA), and together produce a burden of disease that may be equivalent to up to one-half of SSA's malaria disease burden and more than double that caused by tuberculosis'.[1] Some of these diseases do not only affect humans but animals too. Trypanosomiasis, transmitted by the tsetse fly, prevents about one third of the land surface south of the Sahara being used for livestock. It has a specially deadly effect on horses, which ensured that large parts of the continent were unable to exploit that animal. Agricultural productivity in Africa is the lowest in the world and a considerable proportion of any crop is lost to diseases and pests, two of the most notorious of the latter being the locust and the quelea quelea bird.

There are other features of the African environment that have made life at least hazardous and development difficult. Generally speaking soil qualities are poor. Because most of the continent is hot all year round organic material continually decomposes and, as a result, the soils are very old and weathered and plant nutrients are less plentiful. Consequently soil productivity declines rapidly under continuous cultivation, thereby requiring African farmers to operate a high ratio of fallow to cultivated land. There are of course exceptions to these general-isations. Where there are highlands (much of east Africa), there are richer soils which can sustain a wider range of crops and more intensive agriculture. One recent estimate suggests that:

> Fifty five percent of the land in Africa is unsuitable for any kind of agriculture except nomadic grazing. These are largely the deserts, which includes salt flats, dune and rock lands, and the steep to very steep lands. Though these lands have constraints to sustainability, about 30% of the population or about 250 million people are living, or are dependent on these land resources. About 16% of the land has soils of high quality and about 13% has soils of medium quality.[2]

Beyond the production of food an important aspect of economic growth is the opportunity and capacity to move goods. Here also nature has not been kind. Although the African continent constitutes about 20% of the world's land mass its coastline is about 30,000 km (less than half that of Asia for example), meaning that the sea is less accessible. Over long distances the coastline is unbroken by sizeable inlets (there are few natural harbours) and there are relatively few navigable rivers, as most of them are characterised by alternating sections of low gradient and rapids. South Africa, for example, has virtually no navigable rivers. These formidable obstacles to transportation of goods on any scale have ensured that Africa's coastal population densities are the lowest in the world. Some experts have argued (though this is more controversial) that the very shape of the continent, in terms of its north–south orientation, has traditionally made technological transfers, especially in agriculture, between differ-ent climatic zones more difficult than in Asia and Europe.

These are rough and ready generalisations, and certainly exceptions to them can be found, but broadly speaking they appear to be significant. Another kind of evidence which supports the importance of these factors is the population history of the continent. Despite various prejudices to the effect that the poorer parts of the world are over-populated, Africa has been (and indeed is), if anything, under-populated. Even today, with 20% of the world's land mass Africa has 14% of its population, and that figure was quite a bit lower only thirty years ago. To explain this anomaly historians have suggested that famine has been a persistent feature of African history, often having devastating effects leading to the death of as much as a third of populations. It was sometimes caused by locusts or even protracted warfare, but the main cause was drought. These environmental factors shaped not only economic life but social and political life as well. The fragility of population meant that almost everywhere in the continent before modern times population densities remained low. It is generally agreed that population density is one of the key forces bringing about social and economic change. Low population densities were compounded in Africa by difficult terrain, which was a major constraint on transport techniques (even today transport in Africa is more expensive than most other regions of the world). These factors in turn tended to discourage exchange and to reinforce local self-sufficiency and reduce incentives for technical innovation.

It is important to understand that these were (and are) general tendencies. Nowhere are human beings simply the creatures or puppets of environmental forces. Africans have devised all sorts of techniques and practices to deal with the difficulties they confronted. In some cases it is only recently that it has come to be understood in the West that some of these practices, for example the use of herbs or certain kinds of planting technique, made a lot of sense. But is is fair to say, in the words of a very eminent Africanist that:

the ecological inheritance [of Africa] could never have been less than difficult. Africa was 'tamed' by its historical peoples, over many centuries, against great handicaps not generally present in other continents, whether in terms of thin soils, difficult rainfall incidence, a multitude of pests and fevers, and much else that made survival difficult.[3]

Cultures

What kinds of culture were likely to emerge in such circumstances? Needless to say these matters are controversial, not just because, and obviously, people feel strongly about their cultures. But also because, and this is rather less obvious, in Western societies many people are deeply hostile to the idea of 'culture' in any sense. I should add that many Africans (but by no means all) also take this view. I will return to the political implications of this later in this book but for now I simply need to note its effects. This hostility to the idea of culture comes from two sources. One is the idea that culture(s) stand in the way of some idea of universal values. So if we believe in such values (the usual candidate for this role is 'human rights') it seems as if we have to downgrade distinct cultures, especially if they are seen to be incompatible with what we take to be universal. The second worry is that the term culture implies static and unchanging traditions, and lurking behind this worry is the idea that culture implies 'irrationality'. Because in the historical past Europeans often accused Africans of 'irrationality' this is a red rag to a bull, and brings forth the usual litany of accusations of racism, 'Eurocentrism', and so on. My view is that most of these concerns are nonsense. Between individuals there might be different degrees of rationality (possibly) but there are no such systematic differences between groups of people. Of course cultures are not static and unchanging but we can usefully hang on to the word to refer to peoples' deeper orientations towards the fundamental problems of life and how they should organise themselves.

Given these working assumptions perhaps the most striking feature of African culture(s) was their need to deal with the pervasive tension between the abundance of land and the scarcity of people, a tension sharpened by low levels of technological capacity. It is this relationship which has produced some of the features we often think of as 'typically' African. Survival depended on access to land which was treated as a communal good, not in the sense of modern communism, but rather as a resource of the community within which people had rights to produce or gather food. The abundance of land also shaped much of African family life and social structures. The problem was not, as in Europe and some other parts of the world, to ensure that land remained within a family, because almost everywhere land was plentiful. The problem was rather to accumulate the labour to cultivate the land. The result of this was, in many African societies, great competition for women and an intense concern for fertility. African societies were enormously concerned about matters of reproduction and childbirth. As one eminent historian of Africa puts it: 'this African obsession with reproduction later surprised anthropologists familiar with regions where nature was more benign'.[4] Infertility was dreaded and children were an essential part of social status, a source of labour and welfare provision in old age.

Social structures and cultures adapted to these imperatives. The practice of 'bride price', for example, made sense as a compensation to the bride's family for the loss of her fertility and capacity to work. Polygamy was an ideal way of building up households. But such practices also produced characteristic tensions and the historians are quite right to dismiss notions of a 'harmonious' African community. So there were endless disputes about land, partly because different people could have different claims on it. Infertile or older women were often thought to be cursed or suspected as witches. Many African societies used rituals to identify them and they were often expelled from the society or even killed. There were deep tensions between male generations and it is this that seems to be behind the strong stress in African societies on the social dominance of older men. Practices such as initiation rites, age sets, and ritual fighting were ways of disciplining younger men in societies without elaborate technologies or formal institutions.

With very limited capacities to control their environments many African societies made a sharp distinction between the area of cultivation (the cultivated fields, the village) and the wild 'bush'. The bush or the forest meant evil forces, magic and sorcery, and witches who could transform themselves into wild animals. Initiation rituals, which took place in the bush, often symbolised the civilising of the young, ensuring their entry to the human world. These social and cultural features shaped much of African religious belief. Religious institutions of a complex kind hardly existed outside Islamic areas. The kinds of distinction that have become fundamental in Christian Europe, seeing 'nature' as separate from 'God' and humanity as outside nature, were not found in Africa. Low levels of literacy and a lack of written texts precluded the articulation of rigid dogmatic beliefs, so that notions such as 'heresy' could have little meaning. Attitudes to the spirit world were in many ways rather pragmatic and concerned with problems of fertility, prosperity, and communal harmony. African religious beliefs were therefore rather informal and new notions and practices could be adopted if they appeared to be effective, irrespective of their overall consistency in terms of a doctrine. Thus ideas of a 'higher power' (a supreme being) could coexist with all sorts of nature spirits, ancestors, warrior-heroes, and witches, all of whom exercised great influence over both the material world and the world of human affairs.

Such spiritual forces were everywhere in the environment, which is why certain places had to be avoided. Gods and spirits were associated with elements of the physical environment and also concerned with the daily affairs of ordinary mortals. This made it important to acknowledge these spirits through various rituals, sacrifices, or festivals, often at particular times of the year, in ceremonies presided over by appropriate priests. A deep regard for the ancestors understood as a living force has been widespread in African cultures. The ancestors were often understood as intermediaries with higher spirits, to whom respect must be paid, often in the form of representation at festivals or as carved figures in shrine houses. As well as seeing 'nature' as suffused with spiritual forces it did not make much sense in African societies to make the kinds of distinction that are fundamental in Western thinking between 'politics' and 'religion'. Rather, in African societies chiefs and elders generally claimed the esoteric knowledge and ritual abilities needed to intercede with these supernatural beings and bring fertility, prosperity, and security to their followers, and to stave off misfortune, illness, and death. In many African societies if they persistently failed in these tasks they could be abandoned or even killed.

So while the historians are right to scoff at rather romantic notions of a 'Merrie Africa' where people were in harmony with each other and with nature, we should be careful to note (as some of them are not) that there were and (as I shall argue later) are strong communal elements in African life, ways of binding people together which we may see as 'culture' or perhaps simply ways of survival. And as I shall also argue later it is by no means certain that such ways are not worthy of respect, or indeed that others might not learn from them.

Structures

What were the implications of all this for social and political organisation? A great British historian of Africa once wrote that, 'the most distinctively African contribution to human history could be said to have been precisely the civilised art of living fairly peaceably together not in states'.[5] This is overstating it a little but makes an important point, often obscured by the desire to attribute states to (historical) Africa because they are understood to be 'modern'. What is most striking about African communities in the past, and indeed in some ways into the present, is their resilience, their capacity to adapt to new circumstances, and to withstand often considerable hardship. But this resilience has depended more on social capacities than political ones, particularly institutions like states. This resilience and lack of dependence on states rests on three features of African social structures and practices. Firstly, land has remained a fundamental dimension of African life and, in sharp distinction to experience elsewhere, has never been understood as a matter of individual ownership. This does not mean that land is, as is sometimes said, simply communally owned, rather it inheres in family, clan, or lineage groups, who may not dispose of it as they will, but hold it in a kind of trust for the group. The fundamental understanding was that everyone should have access to enough land to produce food, or at least no-one should starve. It should not be thought that such attitudes were incompatible with quite sophisticated management of land, nor that they were not capable of producing great tensions, for example between men and women, and older and younger men, nor that they precluded conflict. Many African societies have had remarkably complex notions of different rights in land and its uses, and such notions and rights often became the object of energetic, sometimes violent dispute. But on balance this kind of system ensured that property remained within the community and prevented its monopolisation by a few individuals.

Closely connected with this feature are families and households. Again these terms have to be understood rather differently from their current meaning in the West. There family has come to be 'nuclear', that is a bond for the purpose of sexual union and child-rearing. Even in the historical past families in Europe tended to be small partly because Christianity insisted on monogamy. By contrast an African household could contain a man, his wives, their children, many other relations, servants, and in historical times, slaves. Marriages were (and to an extent still are) understood as much more than personal relations between two individuals but rather as bonds between households and wider groupings. And whereas marriage in the West increasingly came to be seen as an emotional tie between two (roughly) equals, African marriage has been much more concerned with exchanges of services and rights in people and their energies. This can be understood in a contractual sense as in the notion of 'bridewealth' (sometimes 'bride price'), not a price in the literal sense but compensation to the bride's parents for the loss of her labour. Polygamous marriage was widespread throughout Africa (it has by no means disappeared today) and made possible very large or extended families characterised by a fairly strict separation of gender roles. It does not take a great deal of imagination to see its considerable advantages, in terms of care of the sick, the young, and the orphaned.

To these features we can connect a third, namely law. Much nonsense has been talked in the past that Africans did not 'have law', but like family or property these terms have to be understood in their context. So for example if we mean by law something that requires written records (and all the apparatus of cases that modern lawyers use) then there is no African law. But if we mean something like the regulation of interpersonal relationships (family, property, etc.) then of course African societies had rules. The spirit of these rules was however rather different. African law was characterised by its informality and flexibility and its central purpose was rather the reconciliation of disputes and the restoration of community harmony, than the characteristically Western obsession with identifying and punishing a guilty party. African customary legal practices have tended to put an equal or greater emphasis on the side of the need for restitution. The wronged party not only needs to see what the rules are and how they have been applied but to receive appropriate compensation. But the guilty party must accept the decision as fair and get some assurance that, his fault admitted and recompensed, he will be received back into the community. The important thing to bear in mind here is that because Africans did not think of themselves as isolated individuals but were attached to groups (whether lineages, age sets, or others – see box) disputes between individuals could rapidly turn into destructive group conflicts. As a result the primary focus of African law was to prevent such escalation.

AGE SETS

All societies attribute some significance to age but common in east Africa (and some other parts of the world) have been age sets, men of roughly the same age organised into groups ranked by seniority, with each group having different social roles. New sets are started in ceremonies that move existing sets forward into the next grade. Rights to marry, have children, to participate in ritual activities or fighting are all integrated into this structure. This form of social organisation cuts across forms based on kin or territorial organisation. The transition from boyhood to manhood is often the most significant and usually involves some test of courage and ability to withstand pain. One of the best known examples of this form of social organisation is the Maasai of Kenya and Tanzania who distinguish junior warriors, senior warriors, junior and senior elders all with different social functions. Some groups, for example the Oromo of Ethiopia, have much more complex set structures. Of course these practices have been considerably eroded in modern times but traces of them remain. There has been a tendency to romanticise groups like the Maasai. We should avoid that, but we should also acknowledge social and cultural differences between people.

These forms of social structure and organisation, far from being simple or 'primitive', were often very complex and made it possible to operate quite sophisticated economic and political practices both in the absence of effective states (in the modern European sense) and with relatively primitive technology. This is not a back-handed compliment, a sort of disguised way of saying that Africans can be just as clever or sophisticated as us, but a serious point about social organisation. Social organisation in the West is (or has become) in some ways rather simple. Consider the family, for example, and the terms we have to indicate family members. Beyond immediate kin we only recognise one generation back (grandparents) and one generation forward (grandchildren). We also recognise siblings and their children (uncles, nieces, etc.). At that point our 'kinship terminology', as the anthropologists call it, gives out. No African society has such an impoverished system and almost all have much more complex systems of referring to a wide range of kin. This was necessary of course because people had to be located, and co-ordinated, in the pursuit of various social activities and because written records were not available. Using forms of social organisation then, Africans could build wider economic and political networks well beyond the scale of the family. In matters of trade for example, even over quite long distances, people used ethnic ties, diasporas of various kinds, secret societies, debt bondage, and hostage taking, all of which enabled them to engage in relatively sophisticated economic practices. Part of the difficulty here is that we (in the West) have had difficulty in acknowledging these practices because we find them repugnant.

Likewise in the realm of power and authority, African social forms have also found ways to place some constraints on rulers. At the level of the local community elders lacked concentrated means of coercion and could only exercise power by way of some kind of consultation, the famous African 'palaver', usually a public meeting which everyone could attend and at which isssues were thrashed out by means of exhaustive discussion. Overbearing leaders or chiefs would experience face-to-face community pressure. As a Tswana proverb puts it, 'a chief is a chief by the people'. Amongst larger scale communities the leader's power relied very much on his ability to build up a significant granary or large herd and to wield sufficient authority to commit the community to collective action. If a chief was unpopular, his subjects could often withhold tribute or refuse to follow him. His disgruntled subjects could quite easily abandon a chiefdom, set up on their own in uninhabited land, or else join the community of a neighbouring chief. Political obligation and identity were fairly mobile and fluid. These factors inclined leaders to rule with some restraint. Such constraints on power were often registered in rituals or traditions. Oaths of investiture reminded a chief of his responsibilities to his people. In some communities rulers could be removed if they failed to use their powers in the interests of the whole group. And even though leaders often based their claims to power on special access to the world of spirits they had to contend with other claimants to such occult knowledge. Aggrieved subjects might well turn to witchcraft which also inclined 'big men' to be careful in the exercise of power.

Histories

We can now return to the troublesome question of history with which we started. If we discard the various kinds of celebratory history that are really a kind of politics we can draw some interim conclusions about our two central themes, the state and development. For various reasons states of the modern kind do not find very promising soil in Africa, a point confirmed by the fact that colonial and post-colonial states confronted rather similar difficulties to pre-colonial ones. Indigenous forms of rule remained stubbornly local, often no more than groupings of villages recognising a chief, a 'big man' whose personal qualities attracted followers, and accepting certain traditional customs in regulating their affairs. Large parts of pre-colonial Africa had no experience of states in any sense of that word. To acknowledge these points does not commit us to Trevor-Roper-like silliness about the 'absence of history'. There is no need or space in this book to rebut such assertions with a narrative history. What evidence there is suggests that before European contact the African continent contained a considerable variety of political formations, and many scholars would suggest there was a broad evolutionary pattern of increasing complexity and scale, along a continuum from small bands of hunter-gatherers, and village-based agriculturalists, to more or less militarised chiefdoms and kingdoms, to empires based on production, slave-raiding, and trade.

Part of this broad pattern was advanced by particularly skilful leaders who, in certain conditions, were able to create larger political systems, the famous empires of Ghana or Mali for example (see box).

THE SONGHAI EMPIRE

Songhai was the last of the great empires of Western Africa. Initially centred on the Niger bend it was founded by Sunni Ali Ber who used the river to transport his troops as well as mounted cavalry. The consolidation of his rule enabled him to acquire increasing control over long-distance trade across the Sahara in copper and gold. His own successor was ousted by one of his generals, Muhammad Ture, known as Askiya the Great. An accomplished military commander, he extended the realm through the deployment of slave armies and a rudimentary bureaucracy as well as levying tribute on more distant lands. At its height his empire extended some 2000 km along the Niger valley. A more

THE SONGHAI EMPIRE (*cont.*)

devout Muslim than his predecessor, he made Timbuktu an important centre of Islamic learning. Towards the end of his life however he was deposed by his own sons. But no stable rule of succession was established and the empire was undermined by endless rivalries among the royal family. Songhai's control of the gold trade attracted Moroccan interest, and in 1591 a Moroccan army overcame a much larger Songhai force and brought the empire to an end, though a rump continued to exist. Like previous empires, Songhai left little trace on subsequent historical developments.

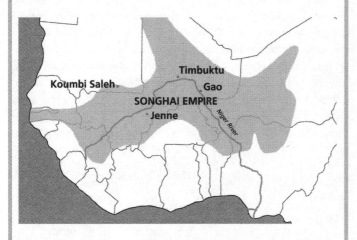

Map 3 The Songhai Empire (image © Roke/Wikimedia Commons)

Such conditions included areas of greater population and wealth perhaps derived from slave labour, control of long-distance trade flows or military force (often allied to some innovations in fighting technique). But these rarely lasted very long and they even more rarely consolidated themselves into more institutionalised systems. The difficulties were considerable and many were rooted in that pervasive tension between land and people that, we have already noted, has so shaped many aspects of African life. Control of land itself (the basis of the Western territorial state) was never central to African polities. Land was almost everywhere plentiful, and given rain-fed agriculture and minimal investment in land, no one piece of it was much more attractive than another. This explains the almost complete absence of map-making in pre-colonial Africa, as the precise demarcation of territorial claims was never at issue. The availability of land, and low population densities, gave the potential subjects of rulers the option to migrate away, a perennial theme in African history, and technological and environmental limitations on the projection of power were also considerable.

That same mobility of populations also proved a major obstacle to the kind of standardisation of customs and culture that is so much a part of what we now understand as national identity. African religious and linguistic pluralism was and remains quite remarkable. Perhaps as many as 1000–2000 languages are still spoken in Africa. More than fifty languages are spoken by more than one million speakers each. Sierra Leone, a country smaller than Scotland, has sixteen mutually unintelligible languages, with four of them recognised as 'national' languages. The power of even larger kingdoms rapidly receded with distance from the capital given the difficulties of transportation. Other forms of state power, for example over currencies, proved impossible to establish. Various forms of money circulated in pre-colonial Africa but none was controlled by a particular polity. Even where larger polities were established, the tendency to polygamous marriage meant rulers produced many male offspring, who were almost certain to contest the succession, and so made the consolidation of dynasties difficult.

However even taking all these factors into account, by the late eighteenth and nineteenth centuries new forms of political rule were emerging in Africa, some of which even European observers at the time reluctantly conceded, had state-like features. These included the forest kingdoms of West Africa (including the Asante and Abomey kingdoms in present-day Ghana and Dahomey), the Fulani emirates of (what was to become) Northern Nigeria or Northern Cameroon, the Tutsi kingdom of Rwanda-Urundi, the Sokoto Caliphate (an Islamic form of state) in Sudan, and the kingdoms of Buganda (in what is now Southern Uganda) and Barotseland (in present-day Zambia). It is striking that many of these emerged in West Africa and the Great Lakes region. Here, as we would expect, trade routes, the productivity of the soil as well as human effort, all contributed to higher population densities, which was conducive to the emergence of more elaborate social and political forms.

Perhaps the two most interesting of these developments were Asante in West Africa and Buganda in the Great Lakes region. The Asante state was a confederacy of major ('paramount') chieftaincies led by the largest, Kumasi, from which the confederacy was ruled by the King or Asantehene. As the Asante expanded their power a large share of the territory and tribute went to the Asantehene and lesser Kumasi chiefs. By the early nineteenth century, the Asante (occupying most of what is now Ghana and parts of Côte d'Ivoire and Togo) had centralised an administration with judicial procedures. The Asantehene established a central authority over all other rulers. An important symbol of this was the Asantehene's reservation to himself of the power to inflict capital punishment. Although the historians argue about the details, the Asante Kings were developing something that looked like a bureaucracy in the nineteenth century, at least a class of officials who were dependent on the King, and chosen for their ability. By the standards of the time the Asante economy was thriving, so much so that even with the ending of the slave trade it was able to adjust and continue trading both to its south and with other polities to its north. The Asante polity even managed to maintain some of the exigencies of economic life, keeping tracks clear through the bush and providing some protection for markets. Some scholars argue that there was the beginnings of the emergence of a commercial class and that this, at least by the nineteenth century, was beginning to have some influence on government.

On the other side of the continent during the seventeenth and eighteenth centuries the kingdom of Buganda had also gradually consolidated. We may note that it developed on a terrain well supplied with rain, and whose elevation ensured that, although located on the Equator, it was never oppressively hot and had excellent soils on its many hills. It was ruled by a Kabaka (King) who exacted tribute from conquered provinces, administering them through a system of appointed officials. Gradually the royal household was expanded into something like an administration. Here was a society with strong historical roots, a form of centralised government, ruling over a territory divided into counties (Saza). The Kabaka levied taxes, appointed chiefs, judged legal cases, waged war, and controlled the distribution of land. He directed an administration which consisted of a Katikkiro, who acted as the Chief Minister, a council of county and department chiefs called the Lukiiko, and several levels of chiefs. Buganda society was structured in a form of clan organisation that was relatively open in terms of social mobility and possessed a capacity to mobilise a relatively large armed force, as all free males could be called on to serve. Nineteenth-century observers encountering the Buganda were greatly impressed by the scale, power, and cultural confidence of their society and commonly referred to it using words like state and nation. As one historian puts it, 'If there existed one nation-state in nineteenth-century black Africa, Buganda would have a good claim to be it'.[6]

The very fact of a more coherent, centralised political organisation in turn allowed some states to sustain a more sophisticated organisation of economic life. The first European visitors to Buganda were startled to complete their journey to the Kabaka's court along a real road, not a track between villages. Asante rulers were known to protect certain markets and maintain trade routes. Probably the most dramatic example of economic growth and sophistication was Kano, the largest town with the most densely populated rural hinterland in West Africa. It was the commercial capital of the Sokoto Caliphate, a leading centre of cotton cloth production, and a crucial hub in a number of long-distance trade networks in West Africa. It was a densely settled city by African standards and, very unusually in pre-colonial Africa, the Caliphate was able to make peasants pay a land tax in the form of cash. This relatively dynamic economy had its own textile industry which in the nineteenth century achieved technical innovations in dyeing and cloth production. We should note however that, as with the adoption of cocoa in West Africa, and the mining and mineral developments in southern Africa, much of this new economic activity relied on coercion. For much of the raw cotton and indigo used in Kano was produced by slaves, who had been imported into the Caliphate as captives from wars against 'pagan' neighbours.

This last point suggests that even when we acknowledge these historical developments we should not romanticise these states, as people have tended to in the past. They were authoritarian, power was often exercised brutally and arbitrarily, and they were usually sustained by constant raiding and wars against other African peoples: 'Ashanti [Asante] is a country for war, and the people are strong', said their ruler in 1820[7] (exactly the same could of course be said about European states a little earlier). The Asante Kingdom was a major supplier of slaves to the Atlantic slave trade until Britain started to suppress it from 1807, one of the paradoxical results of which was an increase in slave holding within the kingdom itself. The leading historian of Buganda suggests that, 'nineteenth century

Buganda was a place of great cruelty and ... the power of the kings rested on systematic violence, both internal and external'.[8]

When Britain decided, in the late nineteenth century, on the conquest of Nigeria, including the Sokoto Caliphate, there was virtually no resistance from the ordinary people of this vast territory. Just as important as the acknowledgement of these facts is to note that even these more developed states were severely limited in their capacity to control their subjects and mobilise resources. They could exercise coercive control and demand tribute, but not much more than that. Warfare was aimed at capturing goods, including people, rather than seizing and holding territory. In the absence of states, determined above all to accumulate wealth and secure the control of land, the relatively harsh environment presented by Africa was bound to impede economic growth. There were other limitations. There was little historical continuity of African states either as structures or as kinds of identity (Ethiopia is the obvious exception). Kwame Nkrumah may well have called his new country Ghana but the old empire of that name was nowhere near modern Ghana nor did it have any great resonance for the people of the new state. There seems little reason to doubt that some of these proto-states, given time, would have started to consolidate into more recognisably modern states. But time, along with much else, was something they were about to lose.

2
Colonial rule and nationalist revolt

Africa first became an object of intense moral concern in Europe as a result of the campaigns against the slave trade which gathered momentum in the late eighteenth century, though their effects continued for long afterwards. But Europeans actually knew very little about Africa itself until well into the middle of the nineteenth century. This was partly because they had to deal with locally powerful groups and rulers, who were not easily coerced, and also because a largely hostile climate, and mysterious but horrifying diseases, were effective barriers to all but the most determined explorers. But these conditions were to change very rapidly in the last third of the nineteenth century, most dramatically in the field of communications. Steamships became larger, faster, and more dependable and were increasingly linked to railway systems at ports. The telegraph revolutionised world communication. By 1872 messages could be sent to Australia. By the late 1880s all of West Africa was linked to Europe. Almost as important were developments in managing tropical diseases and military technology. Although such diseases did not really begin to be understood until the late nineteenth century (the explorer Sir Richard Burton thought that malaria came from sleeping in moonlight) some preventative measures, especially the use of quinine (generally available from the 1850s), were known and increasingly used to good effect, particularly in minimising sickness among European troops. Lastly, this period saw the development of greatly superior military capabilities, in terms of both weapons and military organisation. By the late nineteenth century then, the disparity between the technological capabilities of European states and non-European peoples was the most extreme it has ever been before or since. This contributed to dismissive and culturally arrogant assessments of non-European people and cultures which in turn helped shape an imperial mood.

Such a combination of developments made possible, but did not in itself cause, what is still known in the history books as the 'Scramble for Africa'. The term is something of a misnomer as throughout the nineteenth century large parts of the non-European world, not just Africa, were being conquered by European states. As Cecil Rhodes famously put it, 'I would annex the planets if I could.' It is however true that the conquest of sub-Saharan Africa was remarkably rapid, having started in earnest around 1880 and been completed around 1910, by which time, with the exception of Liberia and Ethiopia, the whole continent was subject to European rule. Two main factors explain the suddenness of the conquest. Firstly, the availability of repeating weapons and light, highly mobile, artillery which meant that African forces could almost always be defeated relatively easily in open battle. Secondly, the fact that much of the fighting was actually done by African auxiliaries because European states were able to exploit differences and tensions both within and between African societies, using recruits from one against the forces of another. The causes of 'the Scramble' were however more complex. Historians still argue about them and they remain politically controversial even today. My own view is that we have to see a variety of factors in play. Nineteenth-century Europe was a place of extraordinary energy and dynamism of which technology was only a part, though an important one. Europeans migrated all over the world, invested all over the world, and conquered all over the world. And they did these things not merely because they could, and not merely driven by self-interest (though that was there too) but because they were certain of their superiority, and their superior civilisation, and felt driven to pass on to others its benefits. As the British Prime Minister Lord Palmerston put it, British imperial rule was 'intended to regenerate the fallen nations of the world and to lift those who had never risen'. These days we find such attitudes so repulsive that we do not even want to contemplate them, but they were normal for the times. Such aggressive societies then encountered much weaker, much smaller-scale ones and the inevitable result was conquest.

The colonial state: bula matari crusher of rocks?

It is of course the violence of conquest and colonial rule that has shaped our sense of colonialism in general and indeed continues to resonate in contemporary politics. A large international gathering in Durban in 2001 issued a ringing declaration denouncing apartheid, genocide, and colonialism as if they were all the same thing, and called on countries to provide compensation for such injustices. And it is not merely those who were at the receiving end of colonialism who have made these impassioned pleas. Various Western think-tanks and lobbyists have demanded that Britain and other colonial powers apologise for the colonial period. So how is it that an enterprise once thought admirable, even noble, has come to be seen, within no more than two generations, as something contemptible, even obscene? It is customary to point to the Second World War and the battles against Nazi doctrines of racial superiority as sounding the death-knell of European imperialism, but this underestimates the impact of the Great War of 1914–18, certainly in the British case. A very large part of the claim to being a superior civilisation had been based on the 'barbarism' of 'backward' tribes and the virtues of imposing order, what Kipling called the 'savage wars of peace'. But in 1914 Europeans began to slaughter each other in huge numbers, often employing and perfecting weapons they had first used in their colonial wars, notably the machine gun. Even before the end of the carnage it was very difficult, at least for more thoughtful people in all sections of society, to believe in claims to 'superiority'. By the late twentieth century such views had generalised into a diffuse, but palpable and widespread, sense of human equality.

It is understandable that this change should be celebrated by those who were once subject to colonial rule, as an expression of regret for injuries inflicted and an affirmation of their standing as part of humanity. We should not however be blind to the very considerable political advantages to be gained in maintaining this account of colonialism, which, as we shall see, has regularly been offered as an explanation of the difficulties of post-colonial Africa. Of course it could only be maintained if it had at least some plausibility. It would be foolish to deny that European colonialism had a very chequered record, which included acts of extraordinary aggression and brutality. It is much more doubtful whether this can be generalised into something like a 'colonial legacy' which explains everything on the continent some fifty years later. We need not reject the idea out of hand but we need to be sceptical about it. It relies on an extremely partial account of colonialism which is not merely historically one-sided, but obscures our understanding of more recent developments, not only but especially the very strong continuities between some colonial practices and attitudes and our own.

But it is fair to give the conventional wisdom its due and start with the bloodier side of colonial conquest and rule. The point has been made that the military technological superiority of European states at this time was overwhelming. That meant that although conquest was relatively easy it also often involved very high African casualties. At the Battle of Shangani River when Rhodes's British South Africa Company attacked the Ndebele army using Maxim (machine) guns for the first time, some 1500 warriors were killed in a matter of hours. Rhodes lost four men. Although there are many similar examples it was not the case that the European powers had it all their own way – there was often determined resistance. In 1879 a Zulu force annihilated a British one of some 1000 men at Isandhlwana (though at terrible cost to themselves). In the Sudan a leader emerged calling himself the Mahdi (Guide) and challenging British rule in Egypt. He had already wiped out a British Egyptian force in 1883. For various reasons Britain did not seek to regain control of the Sudan until 1898 when a fresh army under Kitchener marched against the Mahdi's successor. In a battle at Omdurman lasting some five hours, a British force of 20,000 annihilated an army of 50,000. The Sudanese lost some 10,000 killed as against forty-eight British soldiers. The point is that depite often determined and courageous opposition all over Africa the combination of superior logistics, machine guns, and light artillery proved devastating.

It might of course be argued that casualties are inevitable in war and certainly when modern weapons were used. But on numerous occasions European (including British) forces used violent means that went well beyond the needs of military strategy. Perhaps the most extreme case of such tactics was the massacre of the Herero by German forces in South West Africa. German settlers in South West Africa (now Namibia) had increasingly come into conflict with the indigenous Herero and Nama ethnic groups as they lost grazing land to the settlers. General Lothar Von Trotha, fresh from suppressing a rebellion in German East Africa, arrived with an armed force of ten thousand. The Herero were driven to a point where they were hemmed in by the Germans on three sides. The only available exit was into the Kalahari desert. The Herero were duly pursued into the Kalahari, where water holes were poisoned and guards posted along the one hundred and fifty mile frontier shot all who attempted to return. After the rebellion was completely quelled, the remaining survivors were rounded up and sent to labour camps for the settlers. Overwork, starvation, and disease reduced their numbers further. A census in 1911 showed that some 15,000 remained out of a population of 80,000.

One might have thought that once the conquest of African societies was completed then the more destructive aspects of colonialism would end, but that was often not the case. Colonial conquest was frequently followed by 'pacification' campaigns as some Africans turned to guerilla modes of resistance or groups in more remote regions continued to elude European rule. Because prevailing attitudes about 'civilisation' excluded non-Europeans, the normal laws of war were thought not to apply to them. European forces engaged in practices such as the destruction of property and the killing of prisoners that had begun to be unacceptable amongst themselves. African allies or auxiliaries, like the notorious Abdul Njai, a military adventurer of Senegalese origin who offered his services to the Portuguese and played a major role in the conquest of Portuguese Guinea, were often allowed to seize loot and slaves, even, as in Njai's case, construct, at least for a time, their own mini 'empires'. In all military situations African lives were treated as of little consequence. Winston Churchill, who was a reporter at Omdurman on the banks of the Nile, though he publicly celebrated British victory, privately denounced the 'inhuman slaughter of the [Sudanese] wounded'.[1]

There were also more indirect effects of conquest and rule. In large parts of eastern and southern Africa in particular, conquest allowed European settlement (as in the Namibian case) which invariably involved forcibly removing Africans from their land or restricting them to certain parts of it. The Maasai were forcibly evicted from much of their land between 1904 and

1911. In Southern Rhodesia settlers finally appropriated about half the total land. All over southern and eastern Africa Africans were shunted into 'native reserves' – often (though not always) the worst land. The demands of colonial states for taxes, and the pressure they placed on African populations to produce export crops to generate tax revenue, often disrupted established (and sensible) methods of doing things and worsened the conditions of human life, as with the famines in East Africa in 1898–1900 and West Africa in 1913–14. Colonial regimes often resorted to forced labour to build an infrastructure, especially roads and railways. The Congo–Brazzaville railway for example, some 450 km long, was built through difficult terrain with fairly primitive technology. Around 120,000 African labourers were involved, of whom perhaps some 60,000 perished through poor conditions, epidemics, and accidents. During the First World War none of the colonial powers hesitated to mobilise African manpower, often by very coercive methods, both for support operations and as recruits to colonial armies. It is not surprising that this catalogue of destruction produced terrible effects on African populations and almost certainly population decline.

All these features of colonial conquest and its immediate aftermath appeared at their worst in the Congo. This huge colony began as a private enterprise of the Belgian King Leopold, who employed the explorer Henry Stanley to investigate the Congo Basin, establish preliminary bases, and sign treaties with African rulers. It was Stanley's road-building exploits that earned him the name 'bula matari', crusher of rocks, but that label also came to apply to ruthless methods of exploration and later administration. At the Berlin Conference in 1885 Leopold's claims were accepted by other European states, which endorsed the creation of a so-called 'Congo Free State' under his personal rule. In order to make the colony pay, Leopold had to resort to increasingly predatory forms of extraction of resources that were little to do with exploitation in any capitalist sense and really no more than a form of theft. The demand for commodities such as ivory and especially rubber was met by increasingly vicious methods. European rubber agents and their African employees were rewarded for the amounts of rubber they collected. Inevitably this system encouraged massive violence against Africans – whippings, mutilation, village burning, and the taking of hostages becoming common. This was Conrad's *Heart of Darkness*, as he called his novel which explores the horrors of imperialism. Leopold himself profited handsomely. With increased European demand exports of rubber grew enormously and the King's personal fortune grew with it, much of it being spent on grand buildings in Belgium. The results, needless to say, were catastrophic for this part of Africa. One historian estimates that between 1880 and 1930 the population of the Congo declined by at least a third, perhaps a half.

The colonial state: a civilising mission?

In the face of such overwhelmingly repugnant facts as King Leopold's Congo, how is it possible to give credence to contemporaries' talk of a mission of civilisation? Later developments in the Congo itself suggest some caution here. In the face of the various atrocities taking place there a well-organised, international campaign was mounted to force the Belgian government in 1908 to take control of the colony away from King Leopold and restrain the worst abuses. This campaign was led by people, notably the Englishman E.D. Morel, who were by no means against colonialism in principle, but who took the idea of a civilising mission seriously and eventually placed enough pressure on Western governments that they intervened to force Belgium's hand. The subsequent colonial regime was heavy-handed and paternalistic, but it set up what was probably the best welfare state in colonial Africa. By the late 1950s the population growth rate in the Belgian Congo was around 2.5%. If it is reasonable to blame much of Africa's population decline on the earlier period of colonialism it seems rather unreasonable to deny it some of the credit for growth in the later colonial period.

So even the Congo case suggests that despite the tendency to play down the idea of a civilising mission it cannot be so easily dismissed, and indeed there are some other reasons why we should take it seriously. Firstly, colonial annexation took place against a background of the ending of the (Atlantic) slave trade. This had more or less ceased by the 1870s and it was hoped that the trade in human beings would be replaced by what was called 'legitimate commerce' – at the time the huge increase in European demand for oils of all kinds seemed to offer a promising way forward. However, far from helping to wipe out slavery, in some parts of West Africa better off Africans, merchants, and traders began to recruit slave labour to grow palm oil for sale. It was developments like this that persuaded even sympathetic observers of Africa in the nineteenth century that the continent was so mired in petty despotisms and endemic conflict that it was unable to sustain the minimum requirements of order and commerce, including the 'internal' order needed to finish off the slave trade. Given these circumstances even outside intervention was preferable. The pervasive sentiments of superiority, however repulsive to modern ears, are understandable in the historical context and it is not convincing to see them as (mere) rationalisations of conquest. While it is true that attitudes of racial contempt were widespread in the nineteenth century, particularly, but not exclusively, towards Africans, they co-existed with very strong assertions of human equality even if these were qualified by the notion that some 'races' were more 'advanced' than others. It is true that recent writing on the internal slave trade as well as the institution of slavery (in various forms) in Africa has sought to marginalise the role of colonial states in its abolition. But I think that much of this speaks to current fashion and strains the evidence. The fact remains that, as one British scholar has put it, 'When the colonizers arrived, slavery was endemic throughout the continent; by the time they left, it had been largely eliminated.'[2]

A second, and rather less obvious reason, is the remarkable parallels between colonialism as a civilising mission and Western domestic strategies focused on the disciplining of mass populations within the framework of the nation-state. It is easy to forget that the modern nation-state in the West is a relatively recent creation, crafted with considerable force and ruthlessness. The promoters of 'civilisation' were not necessarily averse to 'tough' methods either at home or abroad, as the history of say the Scottish Highlands, or the treatment of the American Indians, plainly shows. 'Civilising' people certainly did not necessarily mean being nice to them. It meant taking their land, forcing them into the labour market, disrupting, often destroying, their cherished practices and beliefs. The contemptuous rhetoric directed towards the domestic masses at the least rivalled that directed at colonial natives. A historian writing of this period suggests that, 'Religion in general, and the civilising mission in particular, worked to strengthen the distinction between a "cultivated", Christian and philanthropic middle class and an ignorant, heathen, and morally irresponsible mass', but he is talking about Manchester not Africa![3] Both Britain and France, the major colonial powers in Africa, were engaged in a 'civilising mission' at home, and indeed many of the techniques they developed there were quite quickly transferred to the colonies. As a leading historian of France suggests, 'Colonization became the extension and fulfillment overseas of the process of cultural assimilation ... that was turning peasants into Frenchmen inside France.'[4] The colonial craze for railways, and later roads, for example, was not just about being able to move troops in emergencies, and produce to ports, but was also seen as a means of making societies more dynamic. As one enthusiastic British colonial administrator put it, 'roads open up the Country in a wonderful manner and spell moral as well as material progress'.[5] When colonial rule moved into a rather more benign 'welfare' phase after the First World War, less drastic ways of managing (now more 'civilised') mass populations that had been developed at home – trade unions, urban development, organised sport, amongst others – soon found themselves transferred from the home country to the colonies.

There was, finally, an international dimension to these developments. The international system of states which is now so familiar did not really come into existence until the early nineteenth century. It was the framework for the vigorous competition between states for political and economic advantage which led to the extraordinary global expansion of European colonial empires in the nineteenth century. Less well known but no less significant was that those states saw themselves as creating an international order defined by what they called a 'standard of civilisation'. Countries outside that standard were treated as having less than full sovereignty, though they were not necessarily colonies (China for example). Colonial conquest of Africa, though undoubtedly fuelled by Great Power rivalries, also had, from the beginning, an element of international tutelage. At various international gatherings the colonising powers committed themselves not merely to bringing the 'blessings of civilisation' to Africa but controlling the arms and alcohol trades. As we have seen, the notoriously brutal and predatory (private) regime of Leopold in the Congo was eventually terminated through pressure from the major powers, itself in part driven by public agitation. The continuing importance of this international dimension is supported also by the fact that while the tone of nineteenth-century understandings of 'civilisation' jars on twenty-first century sensibilities, if we strip away the paternalism, the often thinly disguised notions of racial superiority and the concerns with Christian conversion, there is a great deal of continuity with contemporary concerns. These concerns, for example about supposedly oppressive cultural practices, are now, however, formulated in a language of 'human rights'.

All these aspects formed the context of colonial rule and left their mark on its practice. It is difficult to generalise, but colonial rule everywhere involved managing the consequences of various tensions. The most fundamental was a tension between the maintenance of order at minimal cost and a commitment to bringing about change. Despite the image of colonial oppression much colonial rule in fact, not least for reasons of limited resources, had to work through local collaborators. But however innovative or conservative colonial administrations were (and they varied enormously) they could not avoid the fact that not only must they deal with the consequences of the direct changes they were trying to promote, but also with those changes they were bringing about indirectly, often indeed somewhat reluctantly. The introduction of Western forms of money and transport, to mention only two of the most obvious, had all sorts of effects which were neither anticipated nor planned, for example in terms of the social mobility of African populations. A final complication here was that both these issues – order and change, the direct and indirect effects of colonial rule – prompted a great variety of opinion not merely amongst those at home concerned with colonial issues, the metropolitan government, business interests, missionaries, but within the colonial administration itself. Colonial officials from a military background (who tended to predominate until after 1914) often had very different attitudes from, say, legal officers, or from officials increasingly concerned with what we would now call development.

Broadly speaking these tensions and debates produced two kinds of colonial administration, though in practice they were all various mixes of the two. In the more conservative type of colonial rule the maintenance of order was the overwhelming priority and often involved close, more or less collaborative, relations with local intermediaries and considerable reluctance to upset local social arrangements. It was this kind of attitude that explains the reluctance on the part of some colonial administrations to really push the abolition of slavery within African societies precisely because it was such an integral part of the social fabric that tampering with it seemed unnecessarily risky. Quite often this type of colonial rule went along with a rather nostalgic regard for elements of pre-industrial society and distaste for many features of British society such as its commercialism and vulgarity. Indeed within certain limits, some colonial officials showed considerable respect, even admiration, for 'their natives', particularly those thought to exemplify the qualities of honour, courage, and manliness. This often had the consequence of a hostility towards, and resistance to, perceived agents of change whether they be European, such as missionaries or meddling lobbyists at home, or Africans who had taken on various aspects of Western culture and were perceived as 'detribalised'. The model of 'indirect rule' fashioned by Lugard in northern Nigeria, in which the Emirs retained their positions, but under British supervision, is the best example of this type (see box).

However, over time this more conservative mode came under pressure to change because the demarcation of the colonial territory and the construction of the colonial state had unavoidable effects. The very idea of a tightly defined territory with an identity of a kind as shown for example by a 'capital'; the physical presence of power, such as colonial buildings; a single system of law (at least 'supreme' rather than 'customary' law); and, in principle, a single currency: all of these prompted some sections of the African population to see things in different ways. Indeed colonial rule helped to bring into existence just

INDIRECT RULE

In a sense all colonial rule was 'indirect' in that colonial powers, given the critical shortage of resources, had to govern through intermediaries. But the idea and system is generally credited to Lord Lugard, the first Governor of Northern Nigeria. In 1903, having defeated the Sokoto Caliphate, he announced to the traditional rulers that 'Every Sultan and Emir will rule over the people as of old time but will obey the laws of the Governor and will act in accordance with the advice of the Resident.' The general pattern followed elsewhere, but not everywhere, in the British Empire was to leave in place Native Authorities administering a treasury, some kind of advisory council, and courts which tried cases according to traditional customs. These institutions operated under the loose supervision of British political officers. This kind of indirect rule was cheap to administer and also tended to reinforce a conservative tendency to see all Africans as part of discrete 'tribes' with their own customs. Some of it was rooted in Lugard's own prejudices about 'europeanised' Africans. It nonetheless papered over the dilemma that the preservation of tradition was ultimately incompatible with the colonial presence. Even before the Second World War informed opinion was coming to the view that the indirect rule system was no longer viable.

such a class of people because, not least for reasons of cost, colonial states found themselves employing 'natives' in lower level posts, initially as court clerks and interpreters, but later as teachers, welfare workers, and minor officials. British administration in Lagos, Nigeria had managed with forty-five African civil servants in 1881; twenty years later there were nearly 1200; by 1921 more than 5000. This growing African middle class, to varying degrees, internalised the values of the colonisers (in matters of language, personal names, modes of dress, marriage practices, and so on). These groups, certainly in the more developed colonies, began to form a sort of 'civil society', providing the basis for independent newspapers, vigorous litigation, and the expression of opinions on, among other things, social and political matters.

Such tendencies, as well as shifting attitudes, prompted the emergence of a more progressive type of colonial administration. This type was committed to an idea of 'development' which clearly reflected metropolitan norms in matters such as wage labour, housing, welfare and family structures, education. It was therefore more disapproving of practices (in the British colonial phrase) 'repugnant to civilisation', such as female circumcision, polygamy, bride price, elaborate funeral ceremonies, widow-hood practices, and took a more positive attitude towards the 'educated African', not necessarily in the sense of someone entitled (yet) to political independence but in the sense of a potential citizen. In this view the 'educated African' was an ally in the work of development, not a 'detribalised' native to be mocked. Strange as it may seem this view was often reciprocated by Africans themselves, who were by no means universally hostile to colonial rule before the Second World War, a fact that also suggests that some scepticism is appropriate as to whether colonial rule was nothing more than oppression.

Many features of the later period of colonial rule bear witness both to the gradual transition towards a more 'progressive' form of that rule and the way in which it was influenced by develop-ments in the metropolitan countries. There was much concern in Britain, for example, in the 1930s and 1940s with questions of maternal and infant mortality. These concerns rapidly trans-ferred to the colonies, which led to the creation of maternity services aimed at the African population. As a result in at least urban areas maternal health showed rapid improvement. In the Lagos region infant mortaility dropped steadily from 296.3 deaths per thousand live births in 1919 to 134.1 in 1929, 127 in 1939, and 104 by 1949. Maternal health services were much in demand by Africans themselves and by the time of independence Nigeria had an impressive network of maternal health centres. Nigerians also enthusiastically demanded Western education. In 1906 there were only 12,000 children in primary schools in southern Nigeria; by 1926 there were over 200,000, by 1957 over two million. By the latter year even the secondary school population had reached 60,000. Even in settler colonies where arguably the African population was subject to greater exploitation there is solid evidence of substantial improvements in welfare. While 130,000 Kenyans were treated in what were called 'native hospitals' in 1920, the number of patients had increased to 500,000 by 1936 and to one million by 1948. One recent study suggests that, in Kenya, 'progress in health care was substantial in the 1920–70 period'.[6]

Colonial legal history provides considerable evidence of efforts to create a modern legal system which would eventually supersede the tactical concessions it was once felt necessary to make to native custom. Even the codification of 'customary law' was not intended to preserve the 'traditional' status quo for ever but to evolve with changing circumstances. As colonial rule consolidated, customary courts were placed under increasing supervision from 'modern' judicial authorities. Colonial bureaucracies, while subject to fairly close political control, were by no means uniform, and different sections of them could and did pursue different agendas. 'Specialist' officials did not necessarily acquire colonial service 'attitudes'. In the realm of education, for example, it is simply not true, as is sometimes asserted, that the objective was the inculcation of a slave mentality. As education for Africans expanded so did the need for curricula and textbooks. Teaching of the humanities raised difficult questions about what was to be taught. While some school textbooks took standard positions about the worthlessness of African history others did not, but were rather keen to inculcate a sense of pride in their traditions among African students (again as potential citizens).

What seems undeniable is that the ideas and practices the colonisers brought with them inevitably helped bring about social change. Colonial rule, then, was much more than domination, it was also the transfer of new forms of social order. In the words of a very eminent British historian:

> In the final quarter of the nineteenth century numbers of African societies braced themselves against change, engaged with it, and even tried to bend aspects of it to their own purposes. But the conditions of the cultural encounter were running against them, and whatever negotiations they managed to achieve within the new dispensation must be seen against the background of a single, blunt fact. British and other European colonialisms incorporated African peoples into the ideological and materialist worlds of Western modernity. All African cultures are still negotiating dialogue with – and within – the implications of that fact.[7]

Cry freedom!

Seen from this perspective colonial rule now looks rather different. Much more than simple 'oppression' or 'exploitation' (though these elements were present too), it was also an attempt (often very tentative) at the wholesale transformation of radically different societies. The effects of this were nowhere more evident than amongst those sections of the African population who had seized the advantages that colonialism had to offer. They achieved this through two main avenues, often but not always connected. One was the colonial education system, whether the missionary schools, or as governments began to intervene more in the field of education, the state school system. The second was state employment. A few African nationalist leaders in the more developed colonies also made their way through journalism or the law. But whatever the avenue all these groups were sharply distinct from the wider population, in their command of the colonial language, and in their personal conduct, which was orientated towards European models of dress, personal conduct, and values. Such Africans were by no means uniformly hostile towards colonialism. Many identified with the most exalted ideals of Western Civilisation. Patrice Lumumba, the fierce Congolese nationalist of the 1960s, had, in the 1950s, heaped praise on Belgium's civilising mission in the Congo.

So what turned this new stratum of African society against colonial rule? On the larger scale the main contradiction of colonialism was becoming more and more apparent. Colonial rule had promised 'progress', both material and moral. But because the colonial administrations had such dismissive views of Africans their timetables of progress were positively glacial, and in any case the resources they provided for its achievement were rather meagre. This discrepancy between promises and achievements seemed less and less defensible (indeed this point was frequently made by colonial officials themselves). But on the human scale this contradiction was directly experienced in the lives of the new African middle class. Those who had made such supreme efforts to adapt themselves to the new world seemed to be permanently excluded from it, or at least condemned indefinitely to be restricted to its lower levels. The Achilles heel of colonialism then was that the very people who had most internalised its promises increasingly came to see it, not as the means to achieve those promises, but as the main obstacle to their fulfilment. The solution to these desperate feelings was a demand for political independence, since with the obstacle of colonial rule removed, progress could be much more rapidly attained. It has become fashionable recently to see this demand as little more than an expression of the self-interest of these groups, indeed colonial officials often suggested as much. But I think this is a mistake. It is of course true that these 'new Africans' saw themselves as discriminated against in the colonial order and as likely to benefit from a new order in a material sense (what modernising elite ever aspired to poverty and self-denial?); but they also felt very keenly the poverty and backwardness of the African mass population and were fired with zeal to do something about it.

Deep resentment of colonial rule then provided the essential fuel for what would become African nationalism. This resentment relied on two big themes. The first, more negative one, identified a clear enemy (always a good tactic in politics), an enemy moreover that could be attacked with the very notions, such as freedom, justice, and equality, that it had brought in its wake, and had proclaimed as the basis of its moral superiority. Not quite as clear-cut but often in the background was a second enemy. Nagging away at the back of nationalist minds was a puzzle as to why the colonialists had been so successful in their conquest and control of Africa. And for many the second enemy which explained this was African traditions broadly conceived. As Nkrumah put it in 1961, the people had to be liberated 'from the bondage of foreign colonial rule and the tyranny of local feudalism'. Twenty years later Samora Machel, the first president of Mozambique would echo him, insisting that 'for the nation to live the tribe must die'. It is true that there were widespread celebrations of 'tradition'. Francophone leaders talked about 'negritude' and the special qualities of African civilisations. Jomo Kenyatta, the first President of Kenya, wrote a book celebrating the virtues of Kikuyu culture. But the real burden of such exercises was the assertion of racial pride and an insistent statement that Africans were as capable of sustaining 'civilisation' as anyone else. What is remarkably absent is the reassertion of, or demand for the revival of, African traditions in any sense. No African nationalist movement expressed any serious wish to return to indigenous traditions. This explains the second and more positive theme in African nationalism, namely, a strong belief in progress, conceived largely in terms of conventional aspirations to economic growth and political independence, and to be achieved largely by emulating the West. Nationalists adopted the main substance of the vision of modernisation (and the idea of the state as its instrument), claiming only that it had failed to produce progress for the mass population due both to racial exclusion and the subordination of the colonial territories to imperial purposes and interests. African governments, unconstrained by both these barriers, would be much better placed to make rapid progress towards the improvement of the lives of all. At its simplest the claim was that independent African governments could do modernisation better than colonial rulers had done.

Ideas may move mountains, but not on their own. African nationalism might have remained a fervent agitation within narrow circles but without any prospect of effective action. What enabled it to break out into the space of 'real' politics and to inspire mass action? Part of the answer lies within Africa itself, the social changes that were occurring, and the new kinds of politics they made possible. Colonial rule, even if only indirectly, had begun to bring about real, if limited, social change even beyond the African middle class. After the railway perhaps the most dramatic instance of this, and certainly much more important politically, was the town. If colonial rule was embodied anywhere it was in the city where power and its symbols were concentrated. With modern towns came large-scale enterprises and with them large-scale employment. Even in colonies with little modern industry, railways and harbours were labour-intensive enterprises. This fuelled a considerable expansion in the urban population. During the period 1939 to 1947 for example the population of Gold Coast's (Ghana) major towns expanded by 50%. Between 1950 and 1960 the population of Nairobi grew from 120,000 to 345,000, Lagos from 250,000 to 600,000 and Kinshasa from 200,000 to 500,000.

Administration of rural areas had to be done with collaborators, but the town brought into being quite different social forces and these could not be contained within the framework of 'indirect rule'. Even before the Second World War, colonial officials were coming to see this and struggling to cope with its consequences. In a different way these developments also made the contradictions of colonialism more acute. Generally, living standards were much higher in towns, even for Africans, and the beginnings of colonial welfare schemes were in towns. Colonial governments made their first faltering efforts to adjust to these developments, allowing then even encouraging trade unionism for example, and engaging in rather basic town planning. But just as they were conceding much more than than they once would have contemplated, so the concessions of colonial rule seemed increasingly inadequate. Africans were beginning to demand full inclusion in a practical sense: equal wages with European employees, equal welfare rights, and so on.

While there was support in rural areas for the nationalist message, the urban areas were the real engine room. Urban Africans had begun flexing their muscles even in the 1930s but after the war there was a wave of strikes: in Dakar (Senegal) in 1945, in Mombasa and Dar-es-Salaam (Tanzania) in 1947, and on the French West African railway system in 1947. Gold Coast was convulsed by a wave of strikes, protest riots, and consumer boycotts in 1947 and 1948. While these actions were often led by trade unions they tended to generalise into more widespread social protest. In this latter aspect the presence of large numbers of young people, eager for change, was critical. The key here, as so often in politics, was to connect people's aspirations for a better material life to more exalted notions, in this context notions such as 'freedom' and 'independence', and to focus those sentiments on a political enemy that seemed to be the main obstacle to their achievement. The crucial development in making this link was the emergence of modern political parties – a process that was pretty much complete in Africa by the mid 1950s. It was political parties that very effectively turned the more abstract themes of African nationalism – resentment of exclusion and aspirations to modernity and progress – into a political currency.

The advantages of these themes in the rough and tumble of the struggle for independence became increasingly apparent. The details of each transition are too complicated to go into here but the common features are clear. They made it possible to inflict the maximum political embarrassment on the colonial powers who, after all, could hardly repudiate their own commitment to notions such as freedom and self-determination. In the nineteenth century it had been possible to counter such arguments and demands for political participation with assertions about racial or cultural 'backwardness', but by the 1930s, and certainly after the Second World War, such arguments were increasingly illegitimate. The colonial powers were thus placed continuously on the defensive; the responsibility for all problems could be placed at their door; and precisely because the nationalists had had little say in government, they had no record of their own that could be subject to scrutiny or criticism. Even where some African participation in government was in place, its shortcomings could be blamed on the obstructionism of the colonial masters. There were political advantages in this kind of nationalism also in the rapidly emerging space of African politics.

In many colonial territories, even though the appearance of unity was maintained, there were severe misgivings among many groups, whether 'traditional', regional, ethnic, or religious (and sometimes all of these), not so much about independence as such or perhaps even modernisation, but about the intentions of those doing the modernising. Indeed, as it became increasingly clear that independence was coming, different groups were jockeying for position and fears of group domination were beginning to emerge. So the concentration on the main enemy, colonialism, as the source of all ills, helped to maintain at least sufficient unity across a very diverse range of social forces. As the Kenyan nationalist Tom Mboya put it, 'Everyone is taught to know the enemy – the colonial power – and the one goal – independence.'[8] Even where demands for independence were led by particular groups, such groups did not attempt to project their own culture and ethnicity as the content of a nationalist message but remained committed to notions of a territorial nation. Thus, both the emphasis on the primacy of colonial repression and the need for its removal, and the stress on progress, however vaguely defined, did much to manage tensions within nationalist movements which were at best rather fragmented and often quite weak.

There would be a price to pay for these political advantages. Although colonial rule did have aspirations to promote change, the need to maintain order, as well as pseudo-evolutionary assumptions about the slow rate of progress possible in Africa, had acted as a major brake on the processes of change. As a result, while colonial rule had disruptive effects on 'traditional' social structures (which some Africans of course experienced as 'emancipation') it did little to fundamentally reshape those structures. At the same time it constructed a central state of a kind that had never existed before, and the nationalist struggle inevitably focused peoples' minds on who would control that state. Colonial states had done little to assuage such tensions (and had sometimes exacerbated them, sometimes intentionally, as part of a 'divide and rule' policy). While the colonial state enemy provided a common focus on the oppressor this did not matter so much. But with the colonial power gone the weakness of African nationalism would become apparent and the task of managing relations between different groups something that could no longer be ignored. Because African nationalism had very little cultural content (it was not the anguished cry of 'a people' with their own sense of identity) it had few resources to fall back on. In 1959 the first Prime Minister of Nigeria, Abubakar Tafawa Balewa, was 'confident that when we have our own citizenship, our own national flag, our own national anthem we shall find the flame of national unity will burn bright and strong'.[9] That confidence, not least in his own country, was to prove tragically misplaced.

Scram from Africa!

Such rather gloomy considerations were of course very far from everyone's mind in the heady atmosphere of the All African People's Conference that assembled in newly independent Ghana in late 1958, at which the Kenyan trade unionist Tom Mboya issued his dramatic demand for the colonialists to 'scram from Africa' (see box).

Long gone were the respectful requests for consultation and limited political participation that had formed the African agenda of the 1930s and early 1940s. Then colonial rulers were still assuming a very leisurely pace of change in their African colonies. They were beginning to talk about development in the 1930s and coming to see that some of the 'traditional' structures that they had maintained in the interest of preserving social order were now an obstacle to that process. One progressive British Governor of Tanganyika in the 1930s reckoned three to four generations of political experience would be necessary before full African participation in the central government could occur. In the event, the colonial rulers (except for the Portuguese) had 'scrammed' by the 1960s. What happened?

African nationalism cannot be the whole answer here. In some parts of Africa, parts of French West Africa and the High

TOM MBOYA

Tom Mboya was one of a number of first-generation nationalists who had a trade union background. He was born in 1930 in what were called in Kenya the White Highlands and educated at Catholic Mission schools, after which he went to college and then trained as a sanitary inspector. In 1955 he was awarded a British Trade Union Congress scholarship to study industrial management at Ruskin College, Oxford. He had already been involved in trade union activities in Kenya and on his return resumed activities in the Kenya Labour Workers Union. He also began to get involved in politics, forming the People's Congress Party. He was one of the first Africans elected to the colony's Legislative Council in 1957. Like many others he was influenced by Kwame Nkrumah and chaired the All African Peoples Conference in Ghana in 1958. He organised a scholarship scheme for Kenyan, then other African, students at universities in the United States. One of the beneficiaries was President Barack Obama's father. In 1960 he joined his party with others to form the Kenya African National Union (KANU) to prepare for negotiations with Britain on Kenya's independence. He became KANU's Secretary General and after independence in 1963 he was elected as an MP for a Nairobi constituency, later becoming became Minister of Justice and Constitutional Affairs, and then Minister for Economic Planning and Development. On 5 July 1969, at the age of 39, he was gunned down in Nairobi. Although nothing was formally proved, suspicion has remained that his death may have been engineered by President Jomo Kenyatta, who feared a political rival. His life and its grim end illustrate many of the themes of independence and post-independence politics in Africa.

Commission territories in southern Africa (Bechuanaland, now Botswana, Basutoland, now Lesotho, and Swaziland) for example, there was very little nationalist agitation. So we have to look at factors outside Africa as well. A good start towards an answer is the Second World War. In the longer term that war had three crucial effects as far as Africa was concerned. Firstly, it left the European powers more or less exhausted and in little condition to assert their previously dominant world role. Secondly, that dominant role was now to be played by two 'superpowers' as they came to be known, the United States and the Soviet Union, both of which, for rather different reasons, were deeply hostile to colonialism. Thirdly, the Second World War was, in important respects, an ideological war, a war, that is, not about conquest of territory or domination, but rather about the principles of social and political order. The Allies went to war, as they constantly said, to defend freedom and equality. These ideas could, of course, easily be turned against colonialism. There were, however, some complications which delayed the effects of these factors until well into the 1950s. Among the Western allies, although American attitudes to colonialism were known, and occasionally led to friction about what the post-war world would look like, there was agreement to shelve consideration of colonial questions for the duration of the war for the sake of unity. This consensus remained in place for some time after the war. On the other hand the Soviet Union remained a very cautious power after the war and did not really concern itself with the colonial world until the middle 1950s, its attention being almost entirely focused on post-war Europe and to some extent China. A final reason was that initially at least, the European powers showed little inclination to give up their empires, and given their own war losses, were much more interested in developing those colonies as part of an economic recovery at home.

By the middle 1950s, however, the forces making for change became overwhelming. It was rather like the foundations of a building being eaten away even though the structure remains in place. Once the structure starts to crumble the building collapses very rapidly indeed. So what were the key developments? The European powers had already been forced to give up their Asian empires, so a whole raft of new states, such as India and Indonesia, added their voices to the demands for decolonisation everywhere. The Soviet Bloc countries started to take an interest in wider global issues and sensed that colonialism was one that could be played to their advantage in the Cold War. As the confrontation with the USSR increasingly shaped American politics the United States came to see colonialism as a potential propaganda weapon and target for communism, and to take the view that is was better to hand over power to 'moderate' African regimes that would be aligned with the West. Finally, the post-war settlement had involved setting up the United Nations, an international forum in which the West's colonial record was increasingly held up to scrutiny and unequivocally denounced. It was in that forum that the world finally condemned colonialism and demanded its replacement by a new set of principles: firstly, nothing less than full independence for colonial territories was acceptable; secondly, no circumstances could justify the withholding of independence from any people aspiring to it; and finally, that independence ('self-determination' as lawyers call it) was to be understood as applying to territories and not peoples, which meant that colonial boundaries could remain in place. These principles were enshrined in a famous United Nations General Assembly resolution in 1960 which not a single state (even the colonial powers) voted against.

In effect this resolution was an ingenious political bargain which ensured that the process of decolonisation in Africa was much more easily arranged than might have been expected. As the riots in the Gold Coast had shown, the colonial rulers no longer had the stomach to hold on to their colonies if that involved real repression and defiance of international opinion. The various schemes to make tropical agriculture more productive, a groundnut scheme in Tanganyika for example, had not proved successful. In any case by the mid 1950s the European economies had revived to a degree no-one had expected even a few years before, and such schemes seemed much less desirable. But the colonial powers did want to depart their possessions with heads held high, and of course hang on to any modest advantages that continuing relationships might provide. For them the easiest transition would be to ensure that colonial territories were taken over by known political forces relatively quickly. For their part the nationalist elites dreaded the thought of raising the issue of who African 'peoples' were and, despite the slogans of pan-Africanism, were desperate to hang on to the existing territories with their established boundaries. They certainly preferred independence with the more or less willing blessing of the old colonial power and, nationalist rhetoric to the contrary, they knew better than anyone how ill-equipped they were to run a modern state and were happy to retain colonial officials at least during a transition period.

There were some complications in this story, the main one being situations where there was a substantial settler population of European origin which was not party to, and not happy with, political bargains struck between the colonial power and African nationalists. So in Algeria and Rhodesia (now Zimbabwe) the transition to independence took a more violent form involving armed struggle between African liberation movements and recalcitrant local (white) governments. Similar in some ways was the Portuguese Empire, where an authoritarian government in Lisbon resisted African demands for greater particpation and then independence and had to be overthrown by force. South Africa was a unique case, being dominated by not one but two European groups – Afrikaners, the descendants of Dutch settlers in the seventeenth century, and English speakers who had arrived particularly since the late nineteenth century. After the Second World War, when South Africa was already effectively independent from British control, the uneasy equilibrium between these two groups was replaced by clear Afrikaner dominance secured by electoral means. Afrikaner governments then proceeded to implement a series of increasingly rigid policies of racial segregation collectively known as *apartheid*. What made the South African situation special was firstly, that it was a local struggle between a minority white and majority black population and secondly, that apartheid encountered an increasingly disapproving international opinion, which led to intense pressure on the white minority to abandon it completely, though this pressure, along with growing militant action by black South Africans themselves, was not successful until 1989.

In one or two other cases also (Madagascar, Cameroon, and Kenya) the transition to independence was held up by violence. But on the whole not only did some forty countries begin their national existence under relatively benign conditions they also encountered relatively favourable conditions in the wider world. To see why, we need to return briefly to the Second World War and its aftermath. This marked a decisive break with the past in both actions and attitudes. The more political aspects of this have already been touched on. In the post-war world the annexation of territory became absolutely unacceptable and states would not recognise it. This was a tremendous protection for weak states against being gobbled up by larger, stronger ones. A corollary of this was that, although many new states, including all the African ones, were weak, they were now to be considered, however unrealistic this might be, as fully established states with full sovereignty. What this meant in practice was that such notions as 'civilisation' no longer applied and the internal policies of states were not a matter for outsiders. Of course powerful states, particularly France, continued to interfere in the affairs of weak (African and other) states, but they did so for reasons of strategic or other advantage, not to alter their internal social and political systems. In practice states were allowed very considerable leeway in the management of their internal affairs. The Cold War confrontation between the USA and the USSR also reinforced these tendencies because what mattered was where African states stood in the conflict, not what kinds of society they governed or even what policies they followed. All these circumstances gave African states, and their leaders, considerable room for manoeuvre.

The economic conditions were also fairly favourable. Some of this was just luck. The post-war global economy was buoyant, entering a long period of growth in the 1950s. In such circumstances raw materials are in demand and markets are lively. It is true that African producers faced increasing competition for many agricultural goods but demand for minerals and prices remained high for a long period. In some cases, though by no means all, the new states had money in the bank (and virtually no debt), and certainly no shortage of ideas as to what to do with it. Colonial economies had expanded fast in the post-war period. The terms of trade were favourable and oil was cheap. African countries even had good rains in the 1950s. Certainly not a matter of luck, on the other hand, were the historically unprecedented volumes of aid that newly independent African states now had access to. This was associated with the greatly increased emphasis on 'development'. Again there was something of a tacit bargain here. On the side of the colonial powers there was an implicit admission that they had done less for development than they might have done and were therefore prepared to put resources into under-developed states, and of course they wanted access to African goods, especially raw materials; on the side of new African states there was access to resources which could be presented as compensation for past colonial misdemeanours but which would also help them to attain rapid economic growth.

Finally, we should note the more elusive but undoubtedly important factor of attitudes towards Africa in the post-independence period. There were a number of aspects to this. The continuing issue of white colonialism and South African apartheid reminded Europeans (and Americans) of their unsavoury past and encouraged increasingly active campaigns against those things by both organisations and states. Americans especially, as they went through the traumas of racial antagonism and the battles over civil rights in the 1950s and 1960s, increasingly identified the struggles of black Americans with a broader indictment of colonialism and the West's historical role in Africa. Partly as a result of these developments there was increasing sympathy for the onerous conditions in which many Africans lived and a much greater willingness to see something done about it. There was, finally, the diffusion of important, if very vague, notions of human equality beyond the realms of intellectuals to a mass public. This made any kind of judgement about other cultures and peoples, particularly in the light of what increasingly came to be seen as the dishonourable period of colonialism, seem offensive, almost unthinkable. This had very positive consequences for African elites which they did not hesitate to exploit. Thus the world's attention was focused endlessly on the iniquities of Portuguese colonialism and South African apartheid but the many episodes of domestic repression or large-scale conflict, including on occasion mass killings, elsewhere in Africa, were largely ignored.

3

Independent Africa: success and failure

Nkrumah had promised in 1949 that with self-government Ghana would be turned into a 'paradise within ten years'. Outsiders were not quite so confident but the general mood was optimistic. The World Bank's Africa experts thought the continent had excellent economic prospects. This did not seem far-fetched. At the time some of the newly independent African states were compared positively to parts of Asia, both in terms of economic prospects and welfare indicators. South Korea for example was widely regarded as a hopeless case. The third poorest country in Asia, it lacked natural resources, almost all its exports were primary products and it depended largely on foreign aid. Indonesia was not thought of in much better terms. It only reached the same level of GDP as Nigeria by the early 1970s. In 1960 infant mortality rates were better in Nigeria than Indonesia.

Thirty years after Ghana's independence these dreams lay shattered. African states had not only failed to achieve their aspirations but in some cases things were worse than they had been in colonial times (and they had been pretty bad). Certainly all the ambitious schemes to transform their economies had come to naught and even the welfare achievements were threatened. In the late 1950s Ghana's GDP was about the same as Korea's. In 2007 Korea's was more than thirty times larger than Ghana's. By the mid 1990s Nigeria's per capita income remained stagnant while Indonesia's had quadrupled; about 60%

of Indonesia's exports were manufactured goods, virtually none of Nigeria's. Between 1975 and 2000 Indonesia's 'dollar a day' poverty declined from 50% to 7%; Nigeria's increased from 35% to 70%. By 2000 Nigeria's infant mortality rate was three times worse than Indonesia's. Politically, African countries remained extremely unstable with well over half of them experiencing severe political violence, and virtually all of them considerable political instability, at some time or other. In some countries widely respected leaders (such as Houphouet-Boigny in Côte d'Ivoire and Jomo Kenyatta in Kenya), with all the prestige of having brought their countries to independence, had managed a kind of consensus system, peacefully co-opting political opposition. But after their departure from office such societies often collapsed into chaos or drifted into greater authoritarianism. To cap it all the one thing that African states had managed very well, maintaining the peace amongst themselves, also started to erode, and relations between African states became increasingly strained. What went wrong?

'Be brief, we have to do in decades ...'

At the dawn of independence things had seemed very different. Government was now conducted by 'new' Africans: precisely the teachers, journalists, doctors, even public officials, who were the products of colonial rule, who felt its indignities and restraints most keenly and were determined to sweep away those indignities and restraints as fast as possible. Not surprisingly their aspirations were sharply focused on economic growth and welfare spending, particularly in the areas of health and education. But African leaders yearned for something more elusive than economic growth and the welfare benefits it would bring (though they are elusive enough!). They also saw it as their task (to quote various documents of the time) 'to combat prejudices, routine, inferiority complexes and the fatalistic spirit'; to place themselves in step with 'evolutionary laws'; to emancipate the 'spiritually and mentally bewitched'; to 'goad [their societies] into the acceptance of the stimuli necessary to rapid economic development'; to 'create a new mentality and way of seeing things'.[1] Julius Nyerere, the first president of Tanzania (the old British colony of Tanganyika), one historian tells us, 'spoke of indigenous religion with an embarrassed smile'.[2] What we can hear in these phrases is both a resentment at being considered 'uncivilised' and a longing to be considered 'modern' in a much broader sense than growth or welfare, important though those things were. So independence opened the door to extremely ambitious programmes of social change, a mesmerising concoction of ideas about science, progress, discipline, themselves all embodied in the form of the modern state. There were often (rather vague) acknowledgements of the need to adjust this vision to local realities, as well as a degree of realism about the obstacles confronting a modernising project in Africa, and even, occasionally, some ambivalence about the relationship between Africa and modernity. But, despite this cautious note, what stands out is a longing for social change 'like jet propulsion', as Nkrumah put it. When the Dutch anthropologist Peter Geschiere visited a remote village in Cameroon in 1971 he found a poster in a government office which read 'Be brief, we have to do in decades what Europe achieved in centuries'.[3]

How were these great goals to be achieved? 'Seek ye first the political kingdom', Kwame Nkrumah had said and, whatever else they may have thought of him, Africa's leaders followed this advice with great enthusiasm. Everywhere the new leaders created what were called 'one-party states', that is, forms of government in which there was one ruling party and open political competition was not permitted. While it is now very unfashionable to say so, they had some arguments on their side. These arguments concerned both politics and development, the two always intricately linked. The new elites were more than aware that, despite the claims of African unity which had made sense as propaganda against colonial rule, their people were divided in all sorts of ways, by religion, region, ethnic group, and different levels of material progress. They feared these divisions were a potential cause of conflict which in turn could become a source of weakness for the new states or even that they could be exploited by outsiders both within Africa and beyond it. They could also make a plausible case that the effects of colonial rule had left a legacy of division (along the lines of 'divide and rule') so that the first order of business of the new states was to create a feeling of national unity. Added to these political points were arguments driven by the idea of development. If the overwhelming challenge was to 'develop', political opposition was a luxury the new states could ill afford. As Nyerere asked, who could possibly be against development? Better surely to concentrate all the (very limited) resources and capacities of the state on the central tasks of expanding the economy and improving the welfare of the people. Another argument was that colonial rule had produced little by way of an African business class, indeed in many ways had actually hindered it. As the material needs of the population were so pressing, it was reasonable in such circumstances for the state to concentrate the bulk of productive resources in its hands, or at the least have a major say in how they were developed and managed.

I am not suggesting these arguments are wholly convincing, or that they were not in part self-serving (we shall see soon that in some ways they were), but they should not simply be dismissed. African states did have very little administrative capacity in the early years and the expectations they had aroused and the tasks they faced seemed daunting. Africans are not the only people in the world to feel that the petty squabbles of party politics can be a distraction from more pressing issues. African societies were highly divided and any sense of national unity was actually rather thin. That such divisions could be exploited by outsiders became very obvious with the Congo crisis of the early 1960s, when some European states appeared to connive at the secession of the province of Katanga from the new independent Congo Republic. As far as development was concerned the African business class was relatively limited, especially in terms of managing large-scale projects. It is rather conveniently forgotten that, at the time of African independence and for some time after, mainstream Western opinion favoured state direction and big projects. Indeed the economic plans which African countries began to implement, in Tanzania, Ghana, and Côte d'Ivoire for example, had often been devised by colonial officials. One of the countries Francophone Africans knew about most, their old colonial master France, had a highly state-directed, and arguably rather successful, economy. So there was enough real substance in these arguments for them to convince a wide range of African opinion and quite a lot of opinion outside the continent as well.

Partly, though by no means only, under the sway of these arguments, virtually everywhere in Africa, political leaders built up one-party states, making all political opposition illegal. Increasingly centralised forms of rule were adopted in which strong presidents, surrounded by small cliques of supporters, usually from their own ethnic group or home region, wielded enormous power. These developments were often reinforced by the creation of 'personality cults' around the leader. Nkrumah called himself Osagyefo, meaning the redeemer, though he was also referred to as Man of Destiny and Star of Africa. Sékou Touré in Guinea was known as the Doctor of Revolutionary Sciences. One African leader, Jean Bokassa, of the Central African Republic, even had himself made into an Emperor, modelling the ceremony on Napoleon's coronation in 1804! As power was monopolised by a small leadership group other political institutions, notably parliaments and political parties (even the ruling ones) became increasingly unimportant, often more or less completely moribund. Peaceful political competition outside the ruling parties, and often inside them, ceased. No African government changed hands as a result of an election before 1991. In some of the more radical African states, for example those that emerged after the collapse of the Portuguese Empire in 1975, single-party mass political organisations were seen as a method of 'mobilisation', essentially spreading the government's message as widely as possible, but even these increasingly atrophied. In many other cases when their founder died they simply disappeared without trace.

Beyond the realm of party politics African leaders restricted or closed down any social organisations that they thought were, or even might become, centres of opposition to their rule. Even those popular movements and organisations that had emerged towards the end of colonialism, and had often played a major role in rousing anti-colonial feeling, were not exempt. So peasant co-operatives, women's groups, youth organisations, and professional associations were rapidly reined in after independence, and forced to toe the 'party line' or disappear. One of the many exaggerations about colonialism is the degree to which it suppressed opinion. In fact many of the colonies, particularly the more developed ones, had a lively and critical African press which also played a major role in the transition to independence. Sooner or later after independence, virtually everywhere in Africa, the press, radio, and television came under state control. It was this that allowed many African leaders to add to the personality cult some claim to intellectual grandeur as well, though as a leading African intellectual scathingly remarks, 'most of the ideological schemas propounded by African leaders were highly idiosyncratic and often so incoherent as to be beyond the comprehension of the propagators themselves'.[4]

With these consolidated states and as part of a developmental but also a broader 'modernising' project, leaders sought to extend the reach of the state into the wider society. How this was done varied enormously from country to country. This extension of state control was most dramatic in the economic field. There were rapid increases in public spending and major increases in public employment. In Ghana the public service expanded by 70% between 1960 and 1965. There were roughly three times as many people on the public payroll in Africa in the 1980s as there had been in the 1960s, indeed the majority of wage earners were state employees. There was a massive proliferation of new laws, policies, and public (or 'parastatal') institutions designed to promote economic development and foster national unity. Laws were passed to regulate investment, trade, and prices, to influence land usage, to provide financial incentives to foreign and domestic investors, and to give citizens preferential access to jobs and assets in the domestic economy. Huge numbers of new institutions were created, ranging from the small and local such as co-operative societies, settlement schemes, and village administrations to the larger and nationwide such as public enterprises, marketing boards, development banks, and many bureaucratic agencies. Much of this activity was concentrated in rural areas, where African states established many new institutions to facilitate control over rural communities and to put pressure on farmers to increase output and productivity.

But this extension of state power was by no means limited to the economic field. Often apparently 'economic' measures also had a social and political dimension (just as they had in colonial times). In many places African states tried to mobilise or dynamise rural people, whom they often considered to be 'backward'. This particularly applied to nomadic and pastoral peoples that many African governments tried to force into permanent locations. Idi Amin in Uganda even tried to force the Karamojong people to wear trousers! In those states that adopted more radical programmes even settled people were forced into collective villages or pressured to join political organisations. At their best such schemes were intended to bring about improvement, and it is all too easily forgotten that they were supported at the time by Western agencies (including some that now talk loudly about human rights). Such was the policy known as Ujamaa in Tanzania (see box).

UJAMAA

The concept and practice of Ujamaa (roughly 'familyhood') was developed within the framework of the Arusha Declaration (1967), Julius Nyerere's blueprint for a Tanzanian socialism which would be distinct both from Western individualism and Soviet-style communism. Part of this thinking involved trying to stitch together what Nyerere thought were the positive communal values of rural African society with the need for more collective forms for the creation and sharing of wealth to overcome the problems of poverty and backwardness. In practical terms this meant that rural Tanzanians should live together in villages rather than in their usual dispersed homesteads, which would make for more efficient use of resources. Ultimately they would take on responsibility for the management of welfare as well as farm collectively, both of which would help to improve their standard of living. Initially Nyerere took the view that Ujamaa villages would be voluntary with only encouragement from the state, but rural Tanzanians showed little enthusiasm for them so that by 1969 only some 400 had been recognised. This led to greater pressure from the state, and by 1973 some two million villagers had been more or less coerced into villages. In 1976 Nyerere announced that all rural people would be required to live in villages. To achieve this considerable coercion was involved though there was little overt resistance. Far from any great economic gains being made from this process, food production fell dramatically (though drought made things worse). It could, however, be argued that Tanzania's political stability owes something to this exercise.

But the considered opinion of a leading contemporary scholar of such things remains compelling:

> The underlying premise of Nyerere's agrarian policy, for all its rhetorical flourishes in the direction of traditional culture, was little different from that of colonial agrarian policy. That premise was that the practices of African cultivators and pastoralists were backward, unscientific, inefficient, and ecologically irresponsible. Close supervision, training, and, if need be, coercion by specialists in scientific agriculture could bring them and their practices in line with a modern Tanzania. They were the problem to which the agricultural experts were the solution.[5]

And at their worst such schemes were a licence for petty corruption, tyranny, and abuse of office by public officials.

As always with Africa we must be careful not to over-generalise. There were a few (not many) exceptions to these trends. In Botswana, the Gambia, and intermittently Senegal some form of multi-party political democracy continued. In some countries, Côte d'Ivoire and Kenya for example, there was a vigorous political contest and some debate within the framework of a single party. In some of the more radical states, Mozambique for example, there was lively discussion within certain limits. Some countries have always had a fairly vociferous and critical press and in some instances a little more respect was shown for local traditions. But overall African states and their ruling elites saw themselves as engaged in modernising their countries as fast as possible with little reflection as to the effectiveness or the local acceptability of the means.

Good times

In the much more pessimistic mood of recent times about Africa it is easy to forget that African states had some achievements to their credit, not least, given their many weaknesses and difficulties, managing to survive at all. Africa's state boundaries have remained stable since colonial times. African states managed relations between each other fairly well. Certainly they occasionally meddled in each other's internal affairs but there was a remarkable absence of cross-border war compared to anywhere else in the world. There was considerable instability at the elite level, and many military coups, but by and large in the first twenty to thirty years of independence, African countries remained relatively free of violent internal conflict, though there were exceptions such as the Nigerian civil war in the late 1960s, and serious communal conflicts in Rwanda and Burundi. As a group of states they conducted a successful diplomacy at the UN and elsewhere to free the African continent from the last remnants of European colonialism, the Portuguese Empire and South African apartheid which, though it was not decisive, was an important contributory factor in their disappearance. But the real test was always going to be in the domestic arena and the central question to be development. Again excessive pessimism has tended to obscure the historical record. There was modest progress across the board at least up until the mid 1970s and in some sectors beyond that. Over the period 1950–75 the rate of economic growth was 2.4% per head, though averaged over 1965 to 1980 it was 1.5% per head (India was 1.3.%). Some countries did much better than that. Kenya sustained 5% annual economic growth in the 1960s and 1970s and between 1968 and 1974 industrial production was growing at about 9% per annum. In roughly the same period the GDP of Côte d'Ivoire doubled. There was even some evidence of structural change in African economies with industrial production expanding at twice the rate of economic growth up until 1973. Although much of this was in mining, manufacturing grew at about 7% per annum between 1960 and 1980. The areas of growth tended to be food processing, beverages, tobacco, and textiles, mostly for the domestic market. Initially at least food production kept up with population growth. Though this growth was achieved largely by extending the area under cultivation rather than by means of technical innovation, there were signs of increasing use of irrigation as well as greater utilisation of fertilisers and tractors.

Sustained economic growth was the basis not only for the transformations that African leaders dreamed of but also the wealth to provide for much enhanced welfare standards for the population. Here again later pessimism has tended to obscure real, sometimes dramatic, changes. For most African governments education was the golden key to progress, and much of their effort went into this sector. Across the continent there were huge increases in enrolment at the primary level and substantial ones at the secondary level. Between 1960 and 1980 the proportion of children in primary school doubled. Some countries did much better than that. In Tanzania primary school enrolment tripled between 1966 and 1976 and tripled again by 1981, by which time virtually all children were attending primary school, though this was at the cost of keeping secondary school enrolment low. In Ghana primary school enrolment tripled between 1958 and 1965. University education also greatly expanded. At the time of independence there were perhaps 25,000 African students enrolled in universities inside and outside Africa. By the mid 1980s it was well over half a million. All this effort undoubtedly had positive effects. Many countries, including the Gambia, Côte d'lvoire, and Senegal in West Africa and Tanzania and Somalia in East Africa, had literacy rates below 10% at the time of independence. Across the continent adult literacy rates rose from 27% in 1960 to 45% in 1990. In Tanzania adult literacy reached 80% by 1981.

In the field of health and quality of life generally African countries also notched up some achievements. There were improvements in diet and calorific intake. By 1990 about a third of rural Africans had access to safe water, up from 10% more or less in late colonial times, and overall some 50% of the population had access to safe water. In the medical sphere also there were improvements, as the number of both doctors and nurses increased, though African countries varied in their approach to health issues. Tanzania concentrated resources on rural health projects, providing some 8000 villages with their own dispensaries by 1978. By then some eight million rural Tanzanians had access to clean water. In Ghana the number of hospitals doubled in the 1960s. Indeed, although there has been some slippage from these achievements as African countries experienced severe economic contraction and severe conflict in the 1980s and 1990s, some achievements have remained and have continued to be built on. Some very serious diseases, river blindness and leprosy for example, have greatly reduced in incidence, often as a result of imaginative strategies involving community volunteers as well as international aid. Immunisation programmes continue to show success as well as such practices as oral rehydration therapy to counter the effects of diarrheal diseases which had killed large numbers of toddlers. By 1970 smallpox had been eradicated from human populations, and other inoculation programmes reduced the incidence of typhoid, tetanus, and yellow fever. In terms of the welfare of the population its sheer growth is testimony of a kind as it was largely the result of falling death rates. Life expectancy went from forty to fifty-two years over the period 1960–90 and infant mortality fell from 284 per thousand to 175, countries in southern Africa tending to do much better than the average figure for sub-Saharan Africa. A continental population of 480 million in 1981 had increased to some 600 million by the end of the decade.

These points made, however, two important qualifications must be acknowledged. The first concerns not so much the absolute numbers of these changes but their depth. The point here is a simple, if somewhat dispiriting one. Although these changes did all occur their overall impact remained fairly modest. If we look at African economies in the colonial period, in the mid 1960s, in the depths of the crisis of the 1980s, and indeed now after some years of renewed economic growth in the continent, certain features are striking. African economies remain low growth and low productivity; they are heavily reliant on the agricultural sector; they are usually dependent on the export of a few unprocessed raw materials (sometimes, as in Angola and Nigeria, only one, with almost no African country having more than three); levels of investment are extremely low and outside investment is limited to particular and lucrative sectors such as mining, with very little connection to the rest of the economy. Investment in infrastructure remains poor and what there is, is often badly managed. This is one of the reasons why transport costs are so high in Africa compared to the rest of the world. All this has in turn impacted on the welfare dimension where improvements, while more impressive than in the economic field, have also in some ways been rather shallow. As Africa's population has continued to grow fast throughout this period, average real income per head has barely increased between 1960 and 2000. Many of the standard health indicators, infant and maternal mortality for example, have stagnated, even regressed, in recent years. While many more children are in school the quality of education they receive is often very poor, taking place in wretched, badly equipped facilities. Even in the good times Africa was not making as much progress as other parts of the under-developed world and in recent years it has become increasingly out of line with trends in the rest of the developing world, never mind the West.

The second qualification concerns the role of the African state in all this. So far I have suggested that most African states took questions of development seriously. There were obvious exceptions, such as the Equatorial Guinea of the notoriously vicious Macias Nguema whose brutality drove away about a third of the tiny country's population (he was overthrown in 1979), or the Central African Empire of Jean Bedel Bokassa, which collapsed into farce when he had himself crowned Emperor (he was also overthrown in 1979). But beyond these rather bizarre cases many serious analysts of Africa would suggest that many, if not most, African elites were indulging themselves and neglecting their own people almost from the beginning of independence. As the radical Frantz Fanon put it, 'scandals are numerous, ministers grow rich, their wives doll themselves up, the members of parliament feather their nests and there is not a soul down to the simple policeman or the customs officer who does not join in the great procession of corruption'.[6] Could it be, then, as the late Nigerian academic Claude Ake often suggested, that the problem was not so much that development had failed as that it had never really been tried? If that were true then suggesting that the relatively successful period in Africa, from roughly 1960 to 1975, was to the credit of African states and their elites would be a mistake. Much hangs on this question and it is not easy, indeed perhaps impossible, to resolve. Why is it so important? Because if African states do not deserve the credit for the early progress then they are part of the problem. But if they do deserve at least some credit, that suggests that the processes of transformation, that they at least claimed to aspire to, were, and are, much more difficult to achieve than they anticipated. The question then arises as to why that might be the case. To approach these questions we have to look first at what happened to the African state.

Stagnation and decline: internal dynamics

We have seen that very soon after independence, right across Africa, the rather hastily erected system of constitutional government put in place by the departing colonial powers was swept away and replaced by a much more authoritarian form of state. We should not be naive or idealistic about this. Authoritarian rule, in itself, is not an obstacle to material progress or the creation of a viable political community, and may even help achieve those goals. Virtually every modern society (including Great Britain) has used coercive methods towards such ends. So the fact that African states used harsh, often repressive, methods does not in itself show that they were not committed to social progress. But there was always the possibility that an authoritarian form of state would be used not so much, or even at all, to secure development for the whole population, but rather to secure and pursue the interests of one group, or even a small clique around a political figure, against the interests of other groups. This is indeed what has tended to happen. The modernising project of African states ran into increasing difficulties in the 1970s and 1980s and the power of the centralised bureaucratic state came to be used more and more in the service of certain groups or elites bent on little more than enriching themselves. This in turn elicited greater opposition from other groups that had little access to the state and its resources. These two processes together moved many African countries towards much greater levels of of political repression and violence.

Why did this happen? This is the most controversial area of analysis and debate about Africa even today. It is worth reminding ourselves first quite how daunting a task many African elites had set themselves. They were committed to political processes around the idea of the nation-state, that is integrating all groups into a common identity that accepted the legitimacy of a central state; and they were committed to economic processes round the idea of a national and productive economy. The hard truth is that, with virtually no exceptions, they have signally failed to achieve either of these. Why? I will argue for the central importance of three main factors. The first I have already hinted at, namely processes of group conflict. The second is the collapse or exhaustion of the economic strategies that African countries had followed in the period after independence. The third is the nature of African political elites themselves.

To make sense of divisions within any society it is useful to make a contrast between those concerning identity (how people see and think of themselves) and those concerning interest (the material conditions of their lives). In real life these almost always overlap. In Africa the salient differences of identity are ethnicity (or tribalism), region, and religion, though not all are present to the same degree; and the differences of interest are between elite and mass. Once again two mistakes are to be avoided. The first is to assume that everything that happens in Africa is somehow a result of 'tribalism'. This is nonsense. But the second, and the more common among supposedly more sophisticated people, is to assume that tribalism or ethnicity is really something else, say class, or greed, or political manipulation by elites. The people who take this view tend to dislike American or French (or any kind of) patriotism as much as they (actually) dislike African tribalism. In reality tribalism is a kind of patriotism and no more difficult to understand. Being with one's fellows provides both security and some degree of emotional warmth. In ideal circumstances different groups can share the same state (Englishmen and Welshmen, Bavarians and Rhinelanders, and so on) with at most minor friction. But such circumstances often do not exist in Africa. Why not?

The new African states inherited the boundaries laid down by colonial rule. The new rulers very clearly insisted, and with good reason, that those boundaries be maintained, and indeed they have been. But this left them with a huge problem because the boundaries of their states were arbitrary in the sense that they had not been devised with the idea of African independence in mind, and they brought together a very wide variety of different groups. This is not, of course, unknown elsewhere in the world. After the unification of Italy in the nineteenth century it was famously said that 'we have created Italy; now we must make Italians'. But the task of 'making Kenyans' or 'making Nigerians' was and is much more difficult. The groups that make up Kenya or Nigeria had no experience of common political life, not even, as with Italy, any sense of a common historical experience or cultural inheritance. The territories now labelled Nigeria or Kenya contain an astonishing variety of peoples, cultures, and languages. As the Nigerian Chief Awolowo famously said, Nigeria is just a geographical expression. These tribal differences are often exacerbated by regional ones. In many African countries particular groups occupy particular territories which they regard as theirs and outsiders as 'strangers'. Relations with 'strangers' may be cordial but they remain 'strangers'. This is often intensified by attitudes towards land that are still very powerful in Africa. As land is usually controlled by groups rather than owned by individuals it can be felt to be part of a group's identity as well as part of its capacity for economic survival. Finally we must take note of religion as a form of social organisation and identity. Traditional African religion tended to be rather supple and flexible in its beliefs and not given to dogmatism, but over long periods of time both Islam and Christianity have come to be very influential in large parts of Africa. Among other things they have had the effect of 'sharpening' identities and polarising politics. Even in countries such as Uganda, where Christianity is overwhelmingly the major religion, divisions between Catholic and Protestant can become a matter of bitter political dispute.

It is not for a moment suggested that these kinds of identity are all there is to politics in Africa, only that they are a very important part of it. But there are also conflicts, or potential conflicts, of interest, though it is not very useful to call them class conflict as social identities are more fluid in Africa than the term class normally implies. The major division here is between very rich elites and a large impoverished mass with a relatively small intermediary 'middle class'. Africa is one of the most unequal regions in the world, with the bottom 20% of the population receiving something like 5% of the total income. The masses are very poor indeed – perhaps 40% of Africans live on less than a dollar a day. Levels of unemployment are extraordinarily high. Because Africa is still experiencing rapid population growth (though the rate of growth is declining) African populations tend to be very youthful, with perhaps 50% of the population under twenty. In rural areas it is true that 'traditional' mechanisms of sharing and mutual aid may alleviate deprivation but these work much less well, or not at all, in Africa's burgeoning cities, which are often little more than shanty towns. Such social facts can interact with identities in complex ways. Tribal groups can resent pressure on their land from outsiders. Almost everywhere in Africa the old generalisations about a shortage of population and a plentiful supply of land are being overturned and this is heightening tensions. The gap between rich and poor is often articulated in religious terms and from time to time religious cults appear which speak to the aspirations of the poor. The often chaotic facts of urban life, and the inability of African states to provide basic social services, or even minimal public order, reinforce people's commitment to their 'primary' social group, their clan or tribe, or home area.

So with the best will in the world the management, and at least amelioration, of these many social tensions would have been very difficult and required great political skill as well as relatively benign environments. Sometimes this has happened, at least for a while. Particular leaders – Jomo Kenyatta in Kenya, Félix Houphouet-Boigny in Côte d'Ivoire, Kenneth Kaunda in Zambia – with the prestige of being 'Father of the Nation' and presiding over relatively prosperous economies, were able to co-opt opponents by generous allocations of public office which in many ways became a licence for self-enrichment (though they sometimes used more unpleasant methods). This often involved a fair amount of ethnic balancing in state employment to reassure smaller groups that their needs and interests were to some extent being looked after. Such leaders also tried to use economic policy as a way of balancing out growth so that all regions benefited. The huge surge in public sector employment did not just concern development strategy, it was also intended to absorb the large number of people coming onto the labour market with some degree of education. So political skill and policy options were undoubtedly a factor. But a lot depended on circumstances, particularly economic circumstances.

What role did economic circumstances play in the failure of African states? It is of course pure speculation what might have happened in Africa had the economic conditions of the 1980s and 1990s been more favourable. African leaders might have had longer time frames, time to learn from their mistakes, and been able to muddle through. But they were not given those circumstances. There were two aspects to this. The first was essentially internal and concerned the exhaustion of the economic model that most African countries had been following; the second was external − factors which we will examine in the next section. What happened to the economic model? Looking back it is relatively easy to answer this question in general terms. The fairly benign economic environment which African countries experienced in the 1950s and 1960s was really a continuation of trends in the late colonial period, that is to say fairly buoyant markets for African raw materials. While that trend continued African economies would benefit and their structural constraints would remain relatively unproblematic. But if those trends changed then African economies would become cruelly exposed to new risks and their limitations would become very obvious. To avoid that it was necessary to move economies away from producing purely raw materials and towards a more diversified range of activities. But this was something African governments signally failed to do.

The harder question is why did they fail? Essentially for two sets of reasons. The first was what economists call macro-economic mismanagement. We do not have to agree with all the assumptions of economists or the strictures of the World Bank to see that if, for example, governments maintain over-valued exchange rates or impose excessive taxation on agriculture this will have damaging effects on their economies. But this conventional wisdom in a way misses the point. African elites, at least some of them, were trying to *transform* their economies, even industrialise them. Historically, industrialising societies have always extracted resources from the agricultural sector. The question is how they do it, and what effective use they make of those resources. So for example African governments tried to increase the productivity of African agriculture by subsidising inputs such as fertiliser, while extracting resources from the sector by paying the peasants less than the market price for their produce. It is true of course that if governments place increasingly heavy burdens of taxation on peasant producers, or give them a smaller and smaller share of the market price of their produce, as many African governments did, then eventually those peasant producers will react, either smuggling their produce elsewhere or ceasing to produce altogether. But much of that 'mismanagement' was an effect of the grander vision. The neglect of agriculture was not simply a 'mistake' but followed from a view that saw industrialisation as the way forward, and history suggests this is not in itself impossible.

So the real problem was the second set of reasons, which concerns the way in which the attempted transition was carried out. The key point here is that, while African governments were aware of the economic challenges they faced, much of the policy they pursued was ill-judged and worse, extremely badly implemented. Consider these observations from a (sympathetic) British journalist writing about Mozambique in 1979:

> a curious sight greets the visitor to a showpiece state farm which the government has established 60 miles west of the capital ... Some 50 new bright red British tractors are lined up outside the farm office, their wheelless chassis propped on blocks and slowly rusting in the humid air of the coastal plain ... Few of these vehicles have broken down for mechanical reasons but because in normal day-to-day use their tyres have been punctured and since farm labourers [do not] have the means or the knowledge to repair inner tubes ... In the case of the state farm tractor tyre punctures are repaired by cannibalising whole wheels from previously immobilised vehicles, a practice which naturally diminishes the number of road-worthy tractors very quickly.[7]

All over the continent governments created state farms or invested in huge projects without proper costings and without sufficient management know-how. African governments had imagined that public investment was the way forward, but this often resulted in the acquisition of technologies which were expensive, uncompetitive, heavily reliant on imports, and had few linkages with the local economy. So the real disaster was that the attempt to secure resources from agriculture to finance import-substituting industry often made conditions worse for rural people, without producing a vibrant industrial sector. Worse still agriculture itself, in this period fundamental to virtually all African economies, either suffered from neglect or attracted the kind of resources that appeared to be 'modern' (as in the tractor example) but on their own were simply a waste of money. This neglect of agriculture in turn came to have very damaging effects. Fertiliser use was barely a third of that of South Asia. The total area under irrigation remained very low, much lower than anywhere else in the world. Food imports into Africa increased by about 200% between 1974 and 1990, and food aid by some 300%.

We can now sketch the political consequences of this particular economic trajectory. As all economic resources came under the control of the state (or at least were heavily directed by it), and as the strategies adopted to effect structural transformation of the economy failed to bear fruit, political elites increasingly despaired of effecting the changes they had hoped to make, and resorted to the use of state power to protect their interests and those of their own group. The economic deterioration from the mid 1970s began to hit the mass population very hard, producing a further decline in welfare but also in the efficiency of the state itself. So for example the declining tax base of many African countries led to reductions in public sector pay, which not only led to a sharp decline in service standards but greatly encouraged moonlighting and corruption. By 1985, the average Tanzanian civil servant's salary was only 25% of its level a decade earlier. This in turn increased the antagonistic tendencies within African politics as other groups felt excluded from both the economic benefits and the political arena. In sum, African elites found it increasingly difficult to manage group relations as the political benefits of anti-colonialism wore off, and their inability to do this was severely sharpened by a worsening economic situation some, but by no means all of which, was of their own making.

Stagnation and decline: external dynamics

Arguments have raged (and doubtless will continue to do so), as to the best explanation of Africa's decline into economic stagnation and political instability after the early promise of independence. On the one hand the terrible disappointments of Africa's independence so far, combined with powerful feelings of guilt about colonialism and racism, have encouraged tendencies to blame all reverses on outside forces, whether 'the colonial legacy', or multinational corporations or malign Western governments or anything, so long as it is not Africans themselves. On the other hand there are those who focus almost exclusively on Africa's shortcomings, real or imagined, oblivious to the operation of other factors. Once people become committed to such standpoints they find it difficult to see any virtue in any other point of view, but it is worth making the effort to make the best sense we can of factors internal and external to the continent.

I have argued that the dynamics that produced the deteriorating situation in many African countries from the 1970s onwards were largely internal to African states. They would have occurred whatever the wider international economic and political circumstances. But it would be foolish to ignore the fact that there were international factors that had damaging consequences for African countries, and often exacerbated the tendencies in African politics which we have identified. In both political and economic contexts some of these factors were intentional and aimed at African states, while others were more the unintended by-product of the workings of international forces. Three factors stand out. The first was the unfinished business of ending colonial rule, including that very peculiar form of it, South African apartheid. Because Britain and France had been prepared to surrender their colonies, and had done so by the 1960s, it is easy to forget that Portugal continued to vigorously defend its Empire and that both white Rhodesians and white South Africans continued to defy both the black majority in their own states and increasingly vehement international opinion. The second factor that caused difficulties, for at least some African countries, were the entanglements of the Cold War and especially the heightened tensions of the period of intensified American global activism after 1980. Finally, having looked at the internal difficulties of African states and their economic strategies, we need to take account of how wider international developments helped to some extent to derail those strategies.

On 3 February 1960 the British Prime Minister Harold Macmillan made his famous speech to the South African Parliament in which he said, 'The wind of change is blowing through this continent, and whether we like it or not, this growth of national consciousness is a political fact. We must all accept it as a fact, and our national policies must take account of it.'[8] This was a fact his audience were extremely reluctant to take account of. Nor were white audiences in Rhodesia or Portugal any more inclined to. When the tide of independence swept Africa these states had done little to oppose it and were even prepared to live with it. But as it came nearer to the borders of southern and South Africa attitudes began to shift, especially as it became clear that the newly independent African states, even those bordering on or within southern Africa itself, were determined to see an end to colonialism. In Rhodesia in 1965 whites seized power from the British government and set up a local white-controlled regime. The Portuguese, facing growing insurgencies in Guinea-Bissau, Angola, and Mozambique, resorted to increasingly aggressive repression. In South Africa, after an attempt at coming to terms with African nationalism, a new government turned, from 1980, to an aggressive policy of 'destabilisation' involving covert attacks on African states that they deemed to be supporting African 'terrorism', and later, support for insurgencies fighting the newly independent (in 1975) states of Angola and Mozambique.

The scene was then set for an extremely damaging confrontation between white-controlled territories and increasingly popular and effective liberation movements, and their regional and continental allies, over a period which lasted from the late 1960s to the collapse of apartheid in 1989. What made it worse was that both sides appealed to their Cold War allies and

the USA and the Soviet Union responded to these appeals in the
context of their broader global confrontation, providing their
respective sides with weapons and other support. Cold War
confrontations had dreadful consequences in another region of
the continent, the Horn of Africa. Because there were no
complications concerning (white) colonialism this took the form
of a much more conventional Great power proxy conflict. Even
here, however, the crucial dynamics were local and regional.
Ethiopia, under Haile Selassie, had been a close ally of the
United States and ran a fairly conservative administration.
Somalia on the other hand, had territorial claims on parts of
Ethiopia, and, under Siad Barre, had not only moved in a more
radical direction but appealed to the Soviet Union for assistance.
The situation shifted dramatically, however, when Haile Selassie
was overthrown and power assumed by an increasingly radical
military regime. The superpowers then switched sides, with the
USSR and its Cuban ally moving to support the Derg regime in
Ethiopia and the USA shifting to support Somalia. This particular confrontation did not end until 1988, and had devastating
consequences for both countries which still continue.

So there is no denying the fact that in both southern Africa
and the Horn Great power politics made things worse, but we
should not assume that African leaders and ruling elites were
somehow no more than the puppets of those powers. They had
their own agendas and were often as adept at manipulating
outsiders as more powerful states were at manipulating them.
While we should note the very damaging effects of these
conflicts it is important to acknowledge also that both the
confrontations with the remaining colonial powers and the
alignments in the Cold War were not wholly detrimental, but
offered a number of African states some political room for
manoeuvre. The confrontation with apartheid, especially,
obscured the degree to which many African states ill-treated
their own citizens. Even the Cold War gave some African states

a space in which to play off the big powers against each other and to reduce the possibility that their own internal policies would come under much scrutiny.

Some countries, notably Angola, Mozambique, and Somalia were very seriously affected by these political circumstances, indeed have yet to recover from them. For most African countries, however, the more damaging international factor was global economic circumstances. We should not forget the importance of environmental and geographical factors at this point, the consequences of which are not entirely beyond human agency, but which nevertheless are not its product and are beyond its control. Over large parts of Africa rainfall declined by about 25% in the period 1960 to 1990, a worse decline than anywhere else in the world. There were severe droughts, partic-ularly the ones that affected the Sahel (a semi-arid belt of land south of the Sahara) in the mid 1980s and southern Africa in the early 1990s. In 1972 Mali lost 40% of its food production and Nigerian groundnut production collapsed to virtually nothing. In many African countries agriculture, fishing, power, and trans-portation depend on rain-fed rivers and lakes. Lake Chad shrank. In Ghana, the drought of 1983–4 caused a massive fall in the level of the Volta river and the Volta Dam lake, as a result of which the power station's output was cut back to 5% of its normal level and power rationing was introduced in Ghanaian cities.

Beyond these environmental factors, the key development was a combination of external shocks and a dramatic shift in global conditions which reversed all the advantages that African economies had hitherto experienced. The most immediate was a 600% rise in oil prices in the 1970s which greatly weakened all non-oil-producing states, especially as their transport systems tended to be hugely road-dependent. By 1980 Tanzania was spending 60% of its export earnings on oil. Of course African oil producers (Nigeria, Gabon, Cameroon) benefited from the price hike and for some other African countries the effects of the oil shocks was compensated by a commodities prices boom in the late 1970s. African economies might have weathered these difficulties as the rest of the world did. But the commodity boom collapsed in 1978. By 1981 coffee prices had halved and the cocoa price had fallen to a quarter of its previous value. Copper prices fell 75% over a decade.

ZAMBIA AND COPPER

Until the mid 1970s Zambia prospered on the back of high prices for copper. The country's copper earnings rose nearly 300% between 1965 and 1974. It rapidly increased welfare spending but neglected agriculture and failed to achieve much economic diversification, despite pouring resources into a large number of state corporations. During the 1980s, when copper prices fell sharply, Zambia's per capita income actually declined by 5% a year. Its external debt reached US$8 billion by 1990. But these external forces, about which Zambia as a country could do little, were hugely exacerbated by nature of the Zambian state. Though in some ways an admirable figure, Kenneth Kaunda's presidential powers were huge and he made all major policy decisions himself. The one-party state stifled debate. The clientelistic nature of the regime ensured not only a huge public sector but a public sector staffed by unqualified and redundant employees. The country's civil service had increased by nearly 300% in ten years from 1963. The government's own Auditor-General reported in 1986 that there was ample evidence of mismanagement of government finances. Increasing political unrest in the country compelled Kaunda to abandon the one-party state and concede multi-party elections, Zambia being one of the first African countries to return to a system of multi-party democracy in 1991.

This downward trend in the prices of tropical products continued for some two decades. International real prices of major tropical agricultural products fell by between 50% and 86% from 1980 to 2002. Among these products, the situation of coffee and cocoa was dramatic. The prices of coffee on world markets, which averaged around 120 US cents/lb in the 1980s, were around 50 US cents in the 1990s, the lowest in real terms for 100 years. Cocoa prices fell by as much as 7% a year between 1977 and 2001. The cotton price was reduced by half between 1997 and 2002, the lowest annual level in thirty years. Coffee and cocoa are key exports for at least fifteen African countries. These price falls had dramatic effects on what economists call the 'terms of trade', that is, roughly how much of what a country exports will buy of what it imports. The terms of trade moved sharply against Africa, which meant African countries had to produce more just to sustain their current level of imports. Even this in itself would not be such a problem but for the fact that African economies, precisely because they are so undiversified, are heavily dependent on imports of basic commodities such as fuel, fertiliser, and spare parts for vehicles.

The results of these global changes for African economies and people were disastrous. During the 1980s GDP per head declined by 1.3% per annum, and in the period 1990–4 to 1.8% per annum. Africa's share of world trade fell from 6% in 1980 to 3% in 2006. African states now faced collapsing revenues to which they often responded by contracting more debt, thinking to tide themselves over their difficulties. Between 1970 and 1976 Africa's public debt increased fourfold. By 1980 this debt had reached US$55 billion and a decade later US$160 billion. As the crisis continued this burden of debt became unmanageable, forcing African states into the hands of international creditors, the World Bank and the International Monetary Fund. At the same time the sharp contraction in their domestic economies squeezed their domestic revenues and forced cutbacks in, amongst other things, welfare spending. This rapidly showed in deteriorating standards of living so that, for example, by the end of the 1980s something like half the African population were living in absolute poverty and most Africans were as poor as they had been at independence. Large numbers of Africans with any training or qualifications worked abroad (some estimates suggest as many as 100,000 between 1960 and 1990). Ordinary people resorted to smuggling, the 'informal' economy, anything to get by.

Of these facts there can be no doubt, but how far can it be argued that Africa was the victim of international forces beyond its control, which, even if not actually intended to harm its economic prospects, nonetheless have that effect? This argument was popular at the time of the onset of Africa's economic crisis and remains so today, especially with African elites and the aid lobby. It is equally vociferously denied by Western states, international organisations, and most economists. As so often, we need to try and discern not only what truth there may be in the argument but also whose agenda it serves. It is understandable that African elites find it preferable to blame others rather than examine too closely their own faults. It is politically convenient for the aid lobby to stress the external causes of Africa's difficulties, because aid is so frequently presented as a kind of compensation for those supposed causes. Equally, Western states are often loath to admit when they put their own interests first and many of them, and most economists, are in thrall to a modern dogma, that everything is to be explained by 'the market'. We can undoubtedly point to cases where external causes did and do have effects. It is well known that commodity markets are extremely volatile (their prices rise and fall rapidly over quite short periods of time) and as virtually all African countries rely on (mostly) unprocessed commodity exports this feature of the world economy hurts them very badly. And even if these effects are not intended in any sense, they are not beyond human control in that one could envisage managing the world economy in a different fashion such that markets were stabilised. Various proposals along these lines have fallen foul, however, of the dogma of the market. More reprehensible are those policies pursued by Western states which involve the large domestic subsidisation of crops which can be grown more efficiently in the tropics. Such crops as sugar and cotton, and beef production, all of which some African countries engage in, have been affected by such subsidies, which ensures that Western countries produce at a level with which African countries simply cannot compete. However, these points acknowledged, one fact stands out which suggests that international factors are not decisive in explanations of Africa's poor growth record. Whatever the negative effects of the international economy, the fact is that all less-developed economies are exposed to them, and that the countries of Asia and Latin America have done better, often, as we saw at the beginning of this chapter, from a lower base. Indeed, African countries have lost markets to Asian ones. Nigeria was for many years the world's largest producer of palm oil. By 1998 Malaysia produced about 70% of world output, Nigeria's production had all but disappeared, and Nigeria now imports palm oil from Malaysia. It is hard to blame this on the structure of the international economy. Malaysian and Indonesian farmers also faced declining commodity prices but they increased their yields. However, one of the main reasons why they were able to do so that was that their governments invested in agricultural research and infrastructure.

4

Conflict, war, and intervention

By the beginning of the 1990s Africa and its peoples were facing very severe difficulties. A combination of adverse global conditions, especially collapsing commodity prices, and very poor economic management had slowed rates of growth. Some African economies were actually contracting. These would have been burdens enough, but to make matters worse many African countries experienced domestic conflict on a far greater scale than ever before, with some states – Sierra Leone, Liberia, Somalia – virtually collapsing. Others – Guinea-Bissau, Rwanda, Burundi, the Sudan – were racked over long periods by severe conflict. Even states such as Côte d'Ivoire and Kenya, once regarded as success stories, suffered severe economic decline, increasing domestic unrest, and internal political instability. Worse still, the constraints that African states had once accepted on their own behaviour towards each other seemed to be eroding. The disintegration of the Mobutu regime in Zaire ushered in not merely a period of endemic instability in that country (now the Democratic Republic of Congo or DRC), which has yet to end, but precipitated open intervention by several African states that came to be known as Africa's First World War.

At the same time the wider world was experiencing its most dramatic changes since the end of the Second World War. For many in the developed North, 1989 will always be remembered for the fall of the Berlin Wall that had for decades symbolised the great divide between the USA and the Soviet Union. But that fall had repercussions around the world, not just in Europe. Most immediately, the end of the confrontation between East and West meant that there was no need to shore up, on the grounds of their anti-communism, unsavoury regimes whose domestic practices fitted very uneasily with the West's own self-proclaimed values. More, the end of the Cold War seemed to promise a 'New World Order' in which many global problems could now be solved, including the problems of Africa. But the idea of a 'New World Order' also greatly strengthened the voices of those who argued that the internal conditions of African countries, and particularly their states, was the problem. This analysis seemed all the more plausible as large parts of Africa descended into violent conflict. How could there be development of any kind without peace and stability? As a result there has been, since the 1990s, a growing willingness to intervene in African states. Firstly, a much greater readiness to intervene in conflict situations, not in pursuit of strategic or material advantages but for the benefit of Africans themselves. Secondly, there is a much greater willingness to impose limitations and conditions on states. Some of these processes are indeed becoming formalised, for example in the legal sphere with the International Criminal Court. Thirdly, there are forms of intervention, the most ambitious ones, which are intended to completely change societies from the inside.

New wars?

The euphoria about a 'New World Order' was rapidly confronted by new and difficult realities, and not just in Africa. Not only did the end of the Cold War apparently usher in a significant increase in conflict both within and between African states, but these wars seemed to be much more vicious and brutal than previous conflicts, and seemed to fly in the face of the rules of war that had been painfully built up since the nineteenth century. The 'liberation movements' (Frelimo in Mozambique, ZANU in Rhodesia/Zimbabwe, SWAPO in Namibia, MPLA in Angola, and so on) that had helped to free Africa from the last vestiges of colonialism, had been recognised as legitimate entities both as to their political purposes and their tactics. They themselves were inclined to abide by the rules of war (in the treatment of prisoners and such matters) and it made political sense for them to do so, because they had an international reputation to defend. The new insurgent movements in Africa however (Renamo in Mozambique, the Revolutionary United Front in Sierra Leone, the Lord's Resistance Army in Uganda, amongst others) deliberately targeted civilian populations and appeared to be driven by struggles for loot and power rather than any political ideals. They had little interest in explaining themselves to the wider world. Their tactics included the use of child soldiers, the imposition of deliberate famine, mass rape, mutilation, and violent rituals, often incomprehensible to Western observers. So striking, indeed, were these features that some analysts coined the term 'new wars' to define what they considered to be a novel phenomenon.

How plausible is the idea of 'new' wars? As so often we have to be alert to the use of social science and policy jargon to authorise certain kinds of politics. There are two aspects to the politics here. Part of the problem is that so much attention had been focused on 'liberation movements' that much else was obscured and ignored. The truth is that for many commentators the struggle against Western colonialism and South African apartheid was the priority, even to the extent of turning a (very) blind eye to what might be going on in the rest of Africa (and indeed within the 'liberation movements' themselves). The unspoken assumption was that to draw attention to such matters would undermine the liberation struggles in southern Africa.

But in fact much of the violence that took place in the Congo, Rwanda, and Burundi for example, in the 1960s and 1970s, had similar characteristics to 'new wars', though this was not much noticed or discussed at the time. Secondly, there is a more recent politics at play, which is a politics of intervention. The promoters of the 'new wars' jargon are also the promoters of intervening in these conflicts, indeed the terminology is partly designed to encourage outside intervention. The argument here is that because these are not 'proper' wars, but really little more than criminal endeavours, the outside world is justified in interfering. Politically, what the notion of 'new wars' does, then, is to delegitimate African conflicts and, by contrast, make legitimate outside intervention.

If we put aside these essentially politically motivated assessments what can we say about conflict in Africa? It is not controversial that there has been a greater incidence of both internal and cross-border conflict in Africa. What have been the main factors in play? The first, and arguably the most important, is the weakening of many African states. As we have seen, the task of nation-state building, the hard business of welding together very disparate groups into something like a coherent political entity, has proved much more difficult in Africa than anyone anticipated. Secondly, the end of the Cold War removed two constraints on African insurgents. Small arms (which despite that label are very destructive) became easily available from many sources and a much more globalised world made it easier for insurgents to sell certain natural resources – diamonds, coltan (an essential element in the manufacture of mobile phones), tropical wood – to fuel their activities. But at least as important, the end of the Cold War removed an ideological constraint. The superpowers and their allies had demanded a certain degree of conformity to their own ideological viewpoints, or at least insurgent movements thought such conformity to be a necessity to secure continuing support. More recently African insurgencies have abandoned such language and have turned to local meanings and expressions which are more difficult for outsiders to make sense of.

THE LORD'S RESISTANCE ARMY

The Lord's Resistance Army was formed after the defeat by the National Resistance Army led by Yoweri Museveni of Alice Lakwena's Holy Spirit Movement in 1987. It is led by Joseph Kony, who claims to be a prophet and whose mission is to overthrow the Uganda government and rule the country according to the Ten Commandments. Despite its apparent Christian inspiration, the LRA has become notorious for many of the characteristics thought to be typical of 'new wars' – the abduction of children, massacres and mutilations, large-scale looting, and destruction of property. Hundreds of thousands of people have fled their homes and many of them live in government camps. The LRA seems to be in part a result of the hostility of the Acholi people (in northern Uganda) towards the Uganda government, but it is in fact the Acholi people themselves who have suffered most from the LRA. They have also suffered from campaigns by the Uganda People's Defence Force against the LRA, for example Operation Iron Fist in March 2002. The LRA, while it has no explicit political message, does seem rooted in various kinds of political resentment in northern Uganda. Since 2005 many of its members have deserted, and it may now be reduced to a rump of fighters whose motives are largely survival and brutality.

Finally, we can point to an increasing tendency on the part of African states to ignore the norms of non-interference they had put into place soon after independence. It is clear that in certain circumstances African states are increasingly prepared to intervene with force in their neighbours' affairs if they judge it to be in their interests. And although African states were suffering serious declines in their economies, their rate of military spending continued to rise, suggesting they were equipping themselves with the means to do so.

We can see these factors at work all over Africa. In Somalia, the government set up by General Siad Barre, after he seized power in a military coup in 1969, was like many others in Africa, initially at least, a modernising regime. Barre reformed the Somali language, introduced legislation to improve the position of women among a number of radical measures, and talked boldly of abolishing clan loyalties (the Somali equivalent of tribalism). But Somalia was also committed to the restoration of territories in the Ogaden (a part of Ethiopia) which it regarded as an integral part of the country. In 1977 Somalia had attacked Ethiopia aiming to recover that territory. Although Somalia had been a Soviet bloc ally, the recent changes in Ethiopia (the overthrow of Haile Selassie in 1974 and the emergence of a radical military regime) encouraged the Soviet Union and Cuba to switch sides from Somalia to Ethiopia. Their military aid proved decisive in repelling the initially successful Somali incursion. From that point Barre's regime increasingly lost prestige, and although relations with Ethiopia were patched up, internal politics became more violent and dominated by a small circle of Siad Barre's family and clan (the Marehan). As Barre's grip on power began to slip he resorted to ruthless manipulation of clan rivalries, which in turn precipitated violent opposition to the regime. Having abandoned the alliance with the USSR he now received support from the West, which became the main financial prop of the regime, used by Barre to reward his circle and his clan. But with the end of the Cold War Western support dried up, the USA cutting off both military and economic aid in 1989. The country began to break up into separate clan fiefdoms, and by 1990 Barre barely controlled anything beyond the capital Mogadishu. Despite last minute attempts to offer some kind of democracy, his government was overthrown in early 1991. Far from this providing any kind of respite however, the various armed factions now engaged in a murderous struggle with each other which not only directly caused considerable loss of life, but indirectly produced conditions that resulted in widespread famine.

Sierra Leone had had one of the fastest growing economies in West Africa. It is rich in minerals (diamonds, gold, chrome, platinum) and has relatively fertile land with good rainfall. By colonial standards it had a good educational system, including the oldest (modern) University in Africa, Fourah Bay College. But it went into severe crisis in the late 1970s. Collapses in international demand for cocoa and coffee slashed rural incomes. The country was heavily indebted, with debt consuming 130% of its export income. Public services, including education, rapidly deteriorated. The health system virtually disintegrated, services only being available to those with private means. Life expectancy by the late 1980s had declined to forty-two. By 1987 the country's education system was catering for less than 30% of the secondary school-age population. These economic difficulties were greatly exacerbated by the Sierra Leonean state. Government in Sierra Leone had been notably corrupt for some years before the country exploded into violence in 1991. The dynamic here was partly ethnic but also generational, in that the increasing impoverishment of the country had deprived its youth of any prospects of education or employment. Sierra Leone's greatest asset, diamonds, turned into its Achilles heel as politicians vied with each other to secure the cash they generated.

Despite attempts by the government, under international pressure, to reintroduce some form of democratic rule, unrest in the country had already led to the formation of the Revolutionary United Front (RUF), a rather shadowy organisation of disaffected youth and students, which 'invaded' Sierra Leone from neighbouring Liberia in 1991. While some have seen this group as a legitimate representative of popular discontent, its exceedingly brutal methods, including widespread mutilation of civilians, extortion, and the sexual exploitation of women, meant that it secured very little popular legitimacy. It funded its activities by looting and diamond trading and had close connections with a rebel grouping in next door Liberia, which was also racked by internal conflicts, not dissimilar in some ways to those of Sierra Leone. Such a group would not have had so much 'success' however, without at least the tacit connivance of a number of other groups, disgruntled politicians and chiefs, even many government soldiers, who found it convenient to support the rebellion for their own reasons. Many government troops were badly paid and poorly equipped and supported. In any case they often shared with the rebels a hostility to established politicians and a feeling that the political elite had betrayed the country. Moreover, for them too the war provided an opportunity to loot and mine diamonds illegally. Many of the rural recruits to the army might equally, under slightly different circumstances, have joined the rebels. During the 1990s successive Sierra Leonean governments and the RUF battled it out with scant regard for the civilian population. Over some ten years of conflict the death toll was probably around 75,000, with some two million people displaced from their homes and some 20,000 permanently mutilated.

Zaire (now the Democratic Republic of Congo) had experienced considerable violence in its earlier post-colonial history, but once General Mobutu had seized power in 1965 it settled down to a fragile peace. From the beginning his regime was venal and incompetent despite occasional shows of nationalism. Aside from deploying a ruthlessly efficient security apparatus, Mobutu entirely neglected the formal institutions of government and regularly looted the state treasury for resources which he used to maintain an extensive patronage network and to disarm potential opposition. Mobutu expertly navigated the currents of the Cold War, presenting himself as a loyal ally of the

US and the West, a bulwark against Soviet-influenced Angola and Congo-Brazzaville. He was frequently bailed out of political trouble by the United States and France and out of economic collapse by the World Bank (again often conveniently forgotten today). He was also a master at manipulating ethnic and other divisions within the country, and, despite notionally conceding to external and internal pressure to allow multi-party democracy, even managed to hang onto power for some years. To do so he increasingly played the game of ethnic politics in the east of the country, threatening both the domestic opposition and the Western powers that without him as figurehead, the country would collapse into ethnic civil war. For a while this worked, France's support remaining unwavering even when its own Ambassador was murdered by Mobutu's troops in 1993.

What brought Mobutu down was the explosion of violence and the ethnic massacres in neighbouring Rwanda in 1994 which sent many thousands of refugees flooding over the Congo border and irrevocably altered the political situation there. By this time the years of misrule had produced horrendous results. The Congo economy actually shrank by 40% between 1988 and 1995. Copper production dropped from a post-independence high of 500,000 tonnes to 50,000 tonnes in 1993. The per capita GDP in 1993 was 65% less than in the period just before independence. Foreign debt amounted to US$14 billion, unemployment was in excess of 70%, and the transport and communications infrastructure had all but disintegrated. The Western powers, even France and the United States, increasingly came to see that Mobutu was part of the problem and that he had to go. The final element was domestic opposition in the form of the AFDL (known by its French acronym Alliance des Forces Démocratiques pour la Libération du Congo-Zaïre), a loose alliance of anti-Mobutu political movements in which Uganda and Rwanda almost certainly had a hand. A leader emerged, Laurent Kabila, who was able to capitalise on widespread resentment of Mobutu, and whose forces, with professional military support from Uganda and Rwanda, rapidly overwhelmed the Congolese army, which in truth made little attempt to resist, looting as it retreated.

However, whatever hopes there might have been that Congo could emerge from conflict, were rapidly eclipsed by the fragility of the alliance that overthrew Mobutu and continuing interference in the country by other African states. Once in government Kabila rapidly constructed an authoritarian regime, dismissed all ethnic Tutsi from office, and ordered all Ugandan and Rwandan officials to leave the country, thus managing to alienate both the major powers and the regional coalition of forces that had helped him overthrow Mobutu. Almost immediately after the ejection of Rwanda and Uganda, fighting broke out in the east of the country, precipitated by a new rebel movement (the RCD or Rassemblement Congolais pour la Démocratie) that was largely an invention of Rwanda. This time other African states, notably Angola and Zimbabwe, intervened to support Kabila, which produced something of a stalemate and a ceasefire in July 1999.

A duty to protect?

War and conflict, however regrettable, might actually be seen as quite normal and indeed have been so in other parts of the world and in the past. We only need to think of the United States in the nineteenth century, and the long historical rivalry between Britain and France, to realise that most modern states that we know today are the result of ferocious conflicts, both internal and external, which have defined borders and reinforced national identities. So why couldn't we, in the words of one American academic, just 'give war a chance'?[1] Some of the reasons we have already examined. African independence came with the blessing of the Great Powers. Colonialism was by 1960 thoroughly discredited (and has remained so ever since). Outside states harboured no ambitions for African territory, and in any case the annexation of territory, quite common until after the First World War, has also become taboo. The old colonial powers, whatever their faults, were understandably keen to claim credit for the newly independent states, and do not wish to see them disappear or collapse into chaos. So although powerful states occasionally interfered in the affairs of weak (African and other) states they did so for reasons of strategic or other advantage, not to alter the internal social and political arrangements of those states. In practice states were allowed very considerable leeway in the management of their internal affairs. All these tendencies were reinforced by the Cold War confrontation between the USA and the USSR which gave African states some room for manoeuvre.

But there are some other important reasons. One is that attitudes in the West to war and conflict generally have been changing. Increasingly, war has come to be seen as immoral in itself; no longer, as it was in the historical past, a legitimate form of statecraft and a means to pursue interests, but only to be used as a last resort, in self-defence against a clear threat. From this viewpoint the pain and suffering produced by war seems all the more unacceptable, particularly if it is disconnected from any political purpose. Intervention to relieve that suffering then becomes a pressing moral obligation. A concern with human suffering in wartime is not, of course, new but it is in fact historically rather recent. Only in the late nineteenth century did the sufferings of ordinary soldiers begin to attract major attention and action, which led to the founding of the Red Cross in 1864 and the various Geneva Conventions regulating the treatment of prisoners of war. Only during the First World War did soldiers get treated like individuals with clearly marked burial places and war memorials. There remained quite definite limitations to this concern until very recently. It was limited to suffering of a non-controversial kind, mostly the treatment of wounded soldiers and prisoners of war; and it was entirely framed as agreements between states and was constrained by states' perceptions of their vital interests. By contrast, attempts in the nineteenth century to limit certain kinds of weapon, for example gas, failed. So the Geneva Conventions worked because their implementation gave no one state a potential advantage over others in a conflict. They also worked because the Red Cross, and similar agencies, carefully abided by a set of rules of impartiality and neutrality. Their concern was wholly focused on human suffering, not the military or political context of that suffering.

More recently however the limitations imposed by sovereignty have come to be questioned. For centuries the world has worked with this idea of autonomous states managing their own internal affairs. This, after all, was precisely what African nationalists were demanding. This understanding was built very clearly into the structure of the United Nations, whose Charter (article 2(7)) specifically forbids general interference in the domestic politics of states. The circumstances allowing the Security Council to sanction such intervention were very carefully defined in Article 39 as being only those of threats to 'international peace and security'. Article 55 of the Charter requires states to respect human rights but provides no sanctions in the event that they do not. But even at the time of the founding of the United Nations the situation was more ambiguous than a literal reading of the Charter suggests. Most obviously, the defeated leaders of Nazi Germany and Japan were not just removed from power but tried for 'war crimes', strongly implying there were ethical norms above states. The post-war occupying powers in those two countries did not just bring the war to an end and ensure a transition to civilian administration, they also tried to change Germany and Japan so that they would not wage war again.

All these arguments, and precedents, have developed more recently into a more fully fledged justification for humanitarian intervention not simply, or even at all, on the old grounds of suffering, but rather on the grounds of human rights. Later in this book I will suggest some reasons to be very sceptical about notions of human rights, but for now it suffices to say that they have widespread support. The crucial point here is that they provide grounds for coercive interventions against states because they connect state sovereignty with an expanded notion of how states should treat their citizens. The thinking is that if states do not treat their citizens in a certain way (observing human rights) then in some sense they cease to be legitimate states. The argument about sovereignty then fades away. Only 'proper' states can have sovereignty. These arguments were being loosely aired during the 1990s but in September 2000 the Canadian government funded the creation of an International Commission on Intervention and State Sovereignty (ICISS) which released a report called 'The Responsibility to Protect'. This argued that when a state is unwilling or unable to protect its population or, indeed, is targeting its own citizens, the responsibility to protect those citizens is transferred to the international community, which may then act with force and without the consent of the state if necessary. It also allows for a whole series of aggressive measures short of armed intervention to be used. The criteria for military intervention include large-scale loss of life, actual or anticipated, with genocidal intent or not, which is the product of either deliberate state action, or state neglect or inability to act, or a failed state situation; or large-scale 'ethnic cleansing', whether carried out by killing, forced expulsion, acts of terror, or rape.

It is important to note that this was just a report and, though much discussed, is in no sense an established doctrine, and it was met with considerable hostility by both the US and Chinese governments of the time. This is partly because, as so often in politics, new understandings raise difficult new questions. The most pressing is, if intervention in conflicts is justified on human rights grounds, which agencies may engage in such intervention? In principle there is no reason why any agency should not be so justified. The British philosopher Bernard Williams once speculated about a world in which Oxfam had an army, which he thought was a good idea! Most states, however, even those which vociferously support human rights, are rather nervous at such a prospect, and wish to limit such a right of intervention to an international agency, most obviously the United Nations. But the UN itself is not outside politics. It is dominated by the Great Powers who have made it very clear that they do not wish to be constrained by any general doctrine of humanitarian intervention, even though they frequently claim to be engaged in it. Many smaller countries are very wary of conceding some general principle of intervention which could become a charter for Great Power interference in their internal affairs. Nonetheless the idea of what is now called humanitarian intervention has established itself.

What does humanitarian intervention actually mean? There is a tendency to identify it with coercive intervention within a state against the wishes of that state, but this is in fact a rather unusual occurrence. It is more useful to think of humanitarian intervention along a continuum of measures of varying degrees of coercion, not always involving armed force. Perhaps the most important of these is the way that international lawyers and Western states have talked about removing the impunity of political figures. Traditionally, because states were sovereign, Heads of State, and by implication other officials, were 'above the law', there being no law, of course, above the laws of individual states. Powerful states have begun to chip away at that position, devising a whole raft of rather informal measures, to bring pressure to bear on political leaders they do not like. These can include travel bans, seizure of assets, use of intelligence information, and so on. Interestingly, all of these have frequently been used in the African context. However, the informality of such measures is precisely what those who are promoting intervention like least about them. They rightly argue that such informal measures are governed by no principles of a strongly binding nature and are too subject to the vagaries of political calculation and self-interest.

What is the alternative? While those promoting intervention have not yet won the war they have won an important battle. There were precedents in Nuremberg but more recently the Great Powers established ad hoc tribunals for Rwanda and Yugoslavia to pursue prosecutions for crimes against humanity and genocide. From these has developed the idea of an International Criminal Court, which was negotiated between states in 1998 and became established in 2002, although a number of important countries, including the United States, have not recognised it. The ICC is intended to deal with four kinds of 'crime': war crimes, crimes against humanity, genocide, and aggression. The Great Powers cannot, however, agree on a definition of the last, so for the time being the ICC only deals with the first three. This new International Court is intended to replace the kind of ad hoc tribunals mentioned above. Despite the enthusiasm in many quarters for this institution we have to remind ourselves of the politics. The ICC is currently investigating four situations, all of them in Africa, and it has issued its first indictment of a head of State, President al-Beshir of Sudan. This gives us a hint as to the politics. It is hardly plausible that Africa is the only place in the world where such crimes (if it is useful to call them crimes) are being committed. This does not mean, as many argue, that institutions like the ICC are no more than a front for Western power. The people that work in these organisations are very serious and committed and we should take them seriously even if we do not agree with them. But the fact remains that such institutions are part of Western power and that

Africa, because it consists of weak states, is an ideal place to experiment with them. It is more useful to see 'Western power' as taking various forms, the familiar ones of military and economic might which it can use to crush its enemies as recently in Iraq or Afghanistan), but also new forms in which some states are to be handled by other kinds of institution such as the ICC. The parallels with the colonial period, indeed the pre-colonial period, are startling and I shall return to them in the conclusion.

An African Renaissance?

These developments did not, of course, go unnoticed in Africa, at least by political elites. The end of the Cold War was not greeted with great enthusiasm in Africa because those elites were well aware that they would lose some room for economic and political manoeuvre. African states are weak and dependent and must adjust to the realities of international politics more than other states and it was clear that, with the collapse of the Soviet Union, the West would become the predominant force in the world. African countries hurried to adapt their politics, at least rhetorically, to the demands of a newly triumphant West. There was, of course, concern in the continent about the new levels of conflict, driven by worries as to its effects, not merely in terms of the suffering involved, but also its economic repercussions and its damage to the reputation of the continent in the wider world. This changing international environment posed serious questions for the structures and viewpoints that African states had adopted on issues both of security and development. After independence African countries had set up the Organisation of African Unity, a continental body designed to enhance Africa's position in the world. The OAU was designed for and in an age of sovereignty and placed a heavy emphasis on the rights of

African states. Occasionally it attempted to mediate conflicts between states, but it studiously avoided any interference in their internal affairs. Although the OAU did not greatly concern itself with economic matters and questions of development, African leaders had by and large subscribed to the view that Africa's economic problems were rooted in the colonial legacy and her role as raw materials producer in the world economy, and that the way to solve those problems was by regional and continental economic integration. Over the years they had produced a series of elaborate documents and commitments to attain such grand objectives. The real problem was that African states paid only lip service to these schemes and made very little attempt to actually implement them.

But by the 1990s Africa's economic collapse and the increasing scale of conflict meant that both these standpoints were wearing increasingly thin, as was the patience of the outside world. The feeling was growing, at least among some African political leaders, that it was necessary to change direction. This mood was driven forward by a group of larger African countries which were inclined to keep the peace in their own 'backyards', partly in their own interests, partly out of a concern for regional stability. These same countries were, by virtue of their size and importance, more active on the diplomatic stage, and more aware of Africa's plummeting reputation in the wider world. The key players here were South Africa and Nigeria, medium-sized countries by world standards and big powers in Africa. During the 1990s both emerged from semi-dictatorial or military regimes, with new leaders recognising that they had to adjust to new global realities. South Africa in particular, capitalising on the successful transition from apartheid and the universal popularity of Nelson Mandela, spoke of an 'African Renaissance', a grand vision of continental renewal. But this rhetoric had to be cashed out in firm proposals which took some years of discussion. The two issues of security and development were (rightly) seen as linked. The outcome of the deliberations was a two-track process of change at the continental level.

One track, which came to be known as NEPAD (New Economic Partnership for Africa's Development), launched in Abuja, Nigeria in 2001, concerned development. The NEPAD documents rehearse a whole range of key principles such as good governance as a basic requirement for peace, security, and sustainable political and socio-economic development; African ownership and leadership, as well as broad and deep participation by all sectors of society; anchoring the development of Africa on its resources and the resourcefulness of its people; partnership between and amongst African peoples; acceleration of regional and continental integration; building the competitiveness of African countries and the continent; forging a new international partnership that changes the unequal relationship between Africa and the developed world; and ensuring that all Partnerships with NEPAD are linked to the Millennium Development Goals and other agreed development goals and targets. What are we to make of these ambitious aims? Essentially, what it meant was that African states were now at least prepared to adopt the West's language of markets and globalisation and link these to improved political stability and the eradication of poverty. Even more simply Africa would put its own house in order with the West's support. How likely were African states to deliver on this promise? The most dramatic initiative within NEPAD was the African Peer Review Mechanism (APRM). This idea is not a new one, as a number of countries and international organisations have been using such techniques of mutual review. The idea is that African states volunteer to be reviewed by a small group of experts which assesses their general standards of governance in terms of recognised international and African standards. A report is made public and suggestions are made as to how the country may improve. There are, however, no sanctions attached to compliance and it is not yet clear whether this device will make much of a difference to the behaviour of African states.

The more dramatic of the two tracks, and certainly the one with greater implications for conflict and security, was the reform of the OAU, which began in September 1999 when the organisation adopted a resolution to transform itself into an African Union, a process which was completed by 2002. Although the AU Charter continues to assert the importance of African sovereignty it added two new elements. One was a more elaborate model and more detailed timetable of continental integration. So the new African Union has equipped itself with a whole panoply of institutions (some yet to come into operation), including a Parliament, a Court of Justice, and continent-wide economic institutions (see box).

But what attracted the most attention was the second new principle, which reserved the right of the AU to intervene in the internal affairs of member states in 'grave circumstances' and in the event of unconstitutional changes of government. These moves, it is fair to say, were not entirely without precedent. In 1997 the OAU had condemned the coup that removed President Kabbah of Sierra Leone and had requested African states not to co-operate with or recognise the military regime that supplanted him. But these precedents were only firmed into principles with the new AU Charter. Neither of these developments, the new AU institutions or the new principles of intervention, was very original. What has happened is that African leaders have concocted a sort of amalgam of the United Nations and the European Union, constructing, on paper at least, an ambitious set of continental institutions, which would enhance both peace and development. There was nothing original about the criteria for 'grave circumstances' either, indeed they were entirely copied from those being bandied about by Western states and various lobby groups, and were explicit in the terms of the newly founded International

THE INSTITUTIONS OF THE AFRICAN UNION

- The Assembly. The main decision-making body, this is comprised of heads of state, and meets at least twice a year.
- The Commission, ten commissioners holding individual portfolios who manage the day-to-day tasks of the AU and implement AU policies. The Commission reports to the Executive Council. The current chairperson is Jean Ping.
- The Peace and Security Council (PSC), set up in 2004. This body can intervene in conflicts to protect the security of the continent. It has fifteen member states, elected for two- or three-year terms, with equal voting rights. The PSC also oversees the establishment of a permanent African security force, the AU Standby Force. It plans to have five or six brigades of 3000 to 5000 troops stationed around Africa by 2010.
- The Pan-African Parliament, begun in 2004 to ensure the full participation of African peoples in governance, development, and economic integration of the Continent. This body debates continent-wide issues and advises AU heads of state. It currently has advisory powers only, but there are plans to grant it legislative powers in the future.
- The Economic, Social and Cultural Council (ECOSOCC). Established in 2005, ECOSOCC seeks to build partnerships between African governments and civil society. It will include African social groups, professional groups, NGOs (non-governmental organisations), and cultural organisations.
- The Court of Justice. In 2004, the AU agreed that the regional African Court on Human and Peoples' Rights would be merged with the Court of Justice. As of April 2008, the two courts had not yet merged.
- The Financial Institutions. The AU charter names three bodies: the African Central Bank, the African Monetary Fund, and the African Investment Bank. Of these, only the African Investment Bank has been established but it is not yet functional.

Criminal Court. They included war crimes, crimes against humanity, and genocide.

How would such interventions be organised? As evidence of the seriousness of their intentions the AU committed itself to a Common African Defence and Security Policy, the centrepiece of which is a Peace and Security Council, which meets regularly and recommends action to the Assembly of the Union. The Peace and Security Council is also mandated to:

> follow up, within the framework of its conflict prevention responsibilities, progress towards the promotion of democratic practices, good governance, the rule of law, protection of human rights and fundamental freedoms, respect for the sanctity of human life and international humanitarian law by Member States.

The PSC may also impose sanctions or take other action against African states in the event of unconstitutional changes of government. A raft of other initiatives or mechanisms have been suggested. These include a Continental Early Warning System (CEWS), a Panel of the Wise, a Peace Fund, and an African Standby Force (ASF). It is fair to say that there is great deal on paper but not as yet much on the ground.

If such scepticism, or at least caution, is warranted, perhaps it is more realistic to place some faith in the capacity of African regional organisations to preserve a degree of security in their respective areas. As at the continental level, regional organisations have been concerned with both security and development issues and have also had a tendency to formulate grandiose plans which bore little fruit. The two most important of these are the Economic Community of West African States (ECOWAS) and the Southern African Development Community (SADC). ECOWAS began life in 1975 as a project of regional economic integration, but latterly its focus has shifted to a more political and security-related agenda. This started in response to the

shifting post–Cold War climate and a revised 1993 Treaty, and
to the increasingly bitter conflicts in the region, for example in
Liberia and Sierra Leone. The Treaty countries reached agreement on a security mechanism in 1999 which in many ways
resembles that of the AU. But some more practical measures
have been or are being implemented, for example trying to
reduce the availability of small arms in the region and the training of troops from across the region in three military schools.
SADC has its origins in the struggle against apartheid and the
need for the African states of the region to show solidarity in the
face of South African destabilisation. Although this gave it some
political coherence it was organisationally weak. With apartheid
gone it reformed itself in 1992 and South Africa became a
member in 1994. The new organisation is similar in structure to
ECOWAS and the AU but like them is stronger on aspirations
than performance. It is not at all clear for example that South
Africa is prepared to surrender its predominant position in the
region (it produces some 70% of the regional GDP).

What then can be made of these attempts in a greatly
changed international environment to deal with questions of
security and development within Africa itself? While of course a
great deal of effort has gone into these new institutions and
significant currents of opinion are keen to see them work, there
are several grounds for scepticism. The first is that it is not at all
clear that the political will exists to make them work and that
even when they do work, at least to some extent, it is because
of the weight of the regional big power. The second is that even
if the political will were there all these institutions are heavily
dependent on outside funding and other kinds of support to
function at all. The military training schools in West Africa, for
example, are bankrolled by the EU. AU missions in Burundi and
Sudan simply would not have happened without outside
funding. Put these two points together and it prompts a third,
according to some observers, which is that these efforts are best

understood as ways to extract resources from foreign donors by speaking the kind of language they will find acceptable. NEPAD abandoned some long-standing African arguments about the causes of weak economic growth and emphasised markets, but the bill for these rhetorical concessions does not come cheap – a suggested US$64 billion a year to come from the West, combining debt relief, increases in aid, and foreign direct investment. All the jargon of human rights, conflict prevention, civil society, and so on comes from the West and as we shall see there are strong reasons to doubt much of its applicability to African circumstances. Finally and perhaps most seriously, these efforts neglect some very deep realities of African states. All experience shows that such ambitious regional and continental organs only really work if they are comprised of strong and reasonably efficient states. West African states can agree on a protocol to track the movements of small arms, but if few of the member countries have the domestic capability to register and monitor the movement of goods, and if in fact many officials in various countries have every interest in conniving at illicit transactions in weapons or other commodities, then such agreements will remain dead letters.

Has intervention reduced conflict?

So far we have seen that there were from the beginning of the 1990s two political processes in play: an increasing willingness in the West to contemplate intervention in Africa's conflicts and a recognition within Africa itself that the continent was under pressure to show it could do more for itself. How did these work out in practice? The best way to make sense of this is to revisit our cases of 'new wars' and see what happened. Somalia was one of the clearest cases of intervention in the literal sense. The country had descended into chaos by the early 1990s, massively disrupting its food system and causing widespread starvation. Politics appeared to have degenerated into faction fighting with no discernible outcome. Western agencies, notably NGOs, started calling for armed intervention, partly in order to get protection for their local and expatriate staff, but also because they generally favoured more muscular involvement. At the same time the United Nations, especially its bureaucracy and its ambitious new Secretary-General Boutros Ghali, saw the opportunity to carve out for themselves a much enlarged global role. The Great Powers, particularly the USA, no longer in thrall to Cold War considerations, were under pressure to 'do something' and it may be that President Bush Senior (who had already lost the presidential election) was thinking of his place in history. He had started talking about a 'New World Order'. This political consensus made it possible for the United Nations to establish a relatively modest mission in Somalia (UNOSOM 1) in April 1992 to facilitate emergency relief and arrange peace talks between the various factions. But the dramatic shift came in November when, whatever the exact reasons (and the experts still argue about them), the USA despatched a large military contingent of some 37,000 men in an operation code-named Restore Hope.

This was the beginning of what is sometimes called 'mission creep'. With predominant force on the ground, and with the immediate humanitarian goals in hand, the UN and the Western Powers began to drift towards a much more aggressive posture in Somalia involving, as the US Ambassador to the UN put it, 'an unprecedented enterprise aimed at nothing less than the restoration of an entire country'.[2] Rather than acting as an umpire seeking to mediate between the various parties to the conflict, the UN forces now began to move aggressively against one party in particular, the forces of General Aideed, whose men had, as it happens, borne the brunt of overthrowing the Siad Barre regime. As a result the UN forces, far from being welcomed as friends, began to be viewed by some Somali factions as part of the enemy. Fighting between UN contingents and Somali groups took place, many Somalis being killed. The UN demonised Aideed and even put a price on his head. The culmination of this increasing antagonism occurred in October 1993 when two US military helicopters were shot down, with the loss of seventeen men (the famous Black Hawk Down episode). Domestic American opinion turned sharply against further involvement and it became clear that the United States had lost the will to remain in Somalia and, having secured the return of its prisoners, began to withdraw. Early in 1994 the UN reduced the scope of its operation to 'traditional' peacekeeping and by March most foreign forces had withdrawn. It is of course easy in retrospect to be critical and see where things might have been done differently. Nor can everything that has happened in Somalia subsequently be blamed on the intervention. Nor is it unreasonable to suggest that in the early phase the UN, by improving food distribution, saved lives. But our main aim in this book is analysis and not blame. From that perspective the striking things about the Somalia intervention are twofold. Firstly, the Great Powers began to deny the legitimacy of the internal politics of some African states. Now they talked about 'gangs' and 'warlords'. African politics was on the way to becoming a social problem a bit like, say, football hooliganism, to be solved by policing and social policies. But, secondly, although this language began to catch on, its implications were by no mean thought through, especially the crucial questions of the scope of such interventions, who would carry them out and how.

These shifts in political direction were very evident in the case of Sierra Leone. By 1996 some six years of conflict had been brought to a temporary end because the Sierra Leone government had hired a professional military force, Executive Outcomes, to secure the capital and the main diamond-producing areas.

This had been remarkably successful and the relative peace established had made it possible to hold elections, won by Ahmed Kabbah. An attempt was made at a political settlement to include the RUF. In May 1997 however Kabbah was overthrown in another coup by a section of the armed forces, and it became clear that parts of the army and the RUF were now colluding more or less openly. The first intervention came not from the West but from a West African force, composed largely of Nigerians under the auspices of ECOWAS. This force overthrew the military regime and restored Kabbah to power. The RUF resumed fighting, seizing Freetown in January 1999 and, while the Nigerians recovered the capital, the RUF remained predominant in the countryside. That predominance had strengthened it politically, and weakened Nigeria's commitment to further intervention so that, after more negotiations, a coalition government was set up in July 1999 which included the RUF and made its leader Foday Sankoh vice-president. This set the scene for the second intervention, this time by the United Nations, brought in to supervise the demilitarisation process that was to follow the peace negotiations. This political settlement lasted only a few months until May 2000, when RUF forces seized UN troops. This prompted a third intervention, now by British troops to rescue UN peacekeepers and jump start the peace process. An enlarged UNAMSIL (United Nations Mission in Sierra Leone) was then able to assist the Sierra Leone government to secure control of the country, leading to the declared end of the war in January 2002, and making it possible to hold elections in May which returned Kabbah to power. There remained, however, a last intervention, this time not taking the form of military force. The government of Sierra Leone requested the assistance of the UN in establishing a special court to try RUF leaders 'for crimes against the people of Sierra Leone' and by early 2001 a draft was agreed, although trials did not begin until 2004.

The circumstances in Congo were different yet again. The assassination of Kabila Senior, who was succeeded by his son Joseph, reopened the process of attempted political reconciliation between the various Congolese factions and the interested regional powers. The RCD had by now split into three different organisations variously connected to Uganda and Rwanda. The military situation was deadlocked as the Kinshasa government could not secure the eastern parts of the country by force, but the rebel movements and their external backers, Uganda and Rwanda, could not hope to overthrow the government by force either. Attempted mediation by the SADC was permanently undermined by the fact that the member states of the organisation took opposing views of the Congo situation. Outside intervention has become much more intense but also more varied and calibrated. Firstly, intense pressure was put by the Great Powers on the main regional actors, Uganda and Rwanda, to withdraw their forces from the Congo. Even though this was supposed to have taken place in 1999 it did not really happen until 2002. Secondly, as the process was constantly disrupted by factional disputes so outside involvement was strengthened by an international committee of ambassadors, as well as considerable financial support for the Inter Congolese Dialogue, enabling the various armed factions, the DRC government, and civil society groups to meet and hammer out an interim constitution, including an agreement on restructuring the army. In effect this very complex and drawn out process was bankrolled by the West. It took some five years to get from an outline agreement to elections that were finally held in July 2006. After a run-off election Kabila won and was sworn in as president in December 2006.

The most substantial form of outside intervention, certainly the most expensive, was the UN mission (known by its French acronym MONUC: Mission de l'Organisation des Nations Unies en République Démocratique du Congo). This began on a relatively modest scale as essentially an observation mission, whose main task was to ensure the withdrawal of foreign forces from the country. However, the withdrawal of those forces may well have precipitated the return to violence in eastern DRC amongst various armed factions. In response the UN has periodically scaled up the MONUC mission to its current level of something like 20,000 troops and an annual cost of US$1 billion. This escalating cost involved not only more UN troops but a change in the way they are deployed, from keeping the peace to aggressive action against certain armed factions and groups, sometimes on its own account, sometimes in co-operation with the Kinshasa government. This greater willingness to use force is evident not only in the UN but in the Great Powers themselves. Although they of course finance the UN operations they have also experimented with new forms of intervention. Sometimes this is connected to their own political circumstances. The European Union for example, or at least the European political elite, wishes to pursue a European foreign policy even though there remain severe misgivings about this within Europe itself. African circumstances provide opportunities where new techniques can be developed in non-controversial settings. In the eastern region of the DRC the EU conducted Operation Artemis in support of MONUC (the UN operation), to give the UN time to strengthen its presence. A second mission, EUFOR DR Congo was conducted in Kinshasa, again in support of MONUC, during the election period, to ensure that elections could take place in a relatively peaceful environment.

There are few general laws in politics and it would be foolish to suggest that interventions in African politics always cause more harm than good. It depends on what is meant by intervention and how it is done. It is interesting, then, to look at the case of Mozambique, the site of a very large UN operation (ONUMOZ) which not only oversaw the termination of bitter conflict but also the country's transition to a new constitution and democratic form of government which has remained stable until today. The first notable point is that the UN intervention was a mediation. Both sides (the Frelimo government and the opposition Renamo) were exhausted and accepted that neither could defeat the other. Before UN involvement there had been protracted negotations between the two parties which had hammered out all the crucial issues (the transition to a new government, the termination of hostilities, and so on). At that point what the Mozambicans needed was help, and this they got in the form of ONUMOZ which was led by a very astute Italian, Aldo Ajello, who kept focused on the politics of the situation. There were no demands for trials as the Mozambicans themselves decided to draw a line under their war, partly because the two main protagonists continued to be the main two forces in electoral politics after 1994 and they had to get along.

What conclusions can be drawn from these various cases about the increasing tendency for outsiders to intervene in various ways in Africa's conflicts? A first step is not to take the claims made at face value and remind ourselves of the politics. It is clear that these various interventions proved to be much trickier and messier than their planners anticipated. Part of this was that nobody really knew how to do them and therefore made it up as they went along. Part of it was that some countries were more concerned about these issues than others and therefore political consensus was difficult to achieve. It is now becoming clear that such interventions are difficult to do and have all sorts of unforeseen effects, that they will be extremely costly and take much longer than anyone anticipated. Already, prominent NGOs are demanding long-term trusteeships be established over certain countries, in effect outside supervision. But underneath all this it is also clear that, as they have developed, these interventions in Africa are not innocent, they are also a project of power. There are no (realistic) demands to intervene against 'human rights abuses' in Chechnya or parts of China. There are no ICC indictments of leaders of the West for their actions against Serbia or Iraq. As a one-time UK Foreign Secretary, Robin Cook, put it, 'If I may say so, this [the ICC] is not a court set up to bring to book prime ministers of the United Kingdom or presidents of the United States'.[3]

A second step is to remind ourselves that politics does not stop in Africa either. African states may be weak and their elites may have to show deference to Western wishes and agendas, but they are not without agendas of their own. We have seen that there is money to be had from intervention. Some African politicians may find it useful to use accusations of war crimes, just as they have found useful accusations of 'terrorism', to undermine their political opponents. These two points prompt a third about historical parallels. From this perspective the period since about 1990 looks much more like some aspects of the nineteenth century than the twentieth, indeed uncannily so. If we set aside certain obvious differences (the contemporary use of human rights jargon, the nineteenth century's concern with Christian conversion) the parallels are remarkable. There is the view that conflict is part of the problem; that such conflict is rooted in the social order; and that not only is intervention justified to bring conflict to an end but it is justified in order to secure the extension of 'civilisation' (what we said then) or 'human rights' (what we say now) to all those who do not yet enjoy them. Of course in the nineteenth century much of this co-existed with (now painful) assumptions of racial superiority, but much else is reminiscent of contemporary debate on these matters.

5
Can outsiders change Africa?

There can be no doubt about the increasing willingness of the outside world to intervene in Africa's conflicts – currently the largest United Nations mission in the world is in the Democratic Republic of Congo. But many of those voices calling loudly for intervention don't merely have in mind intervention to prevent conflict but also believe that it is the duty of other states (and perhaps not only states) to intervene to prevent the conditions that cause conflict. The best way of making sense of this is to briefly return to a distinction we have already encountered, between humanitarian intervention and the idea of 'human rights'. Humanitarianism is a very old idea and conjures up notions of sympathy, empathy, charity, and the relief of suffering without concern for its causes but only for its victims. Its primary purpose is to improve the lives of others at least in the sense of relieving immediate suffering, though it sometimes makes us feel good too. This is the idea that lies behind such things as food aid, debt relief, and intervention to prevent conflict. But for many of those closely involved in Africa not only is humanitarianism not enough, in some ways it is quite wrong. The relief of suffering, in their view, does nothing to confront the causes of that suffering and ensure that it disappears for ever. Almost as bad, it implies a condescension, even an arrogance, towards those whose suffering is being relieved. *We* are doing it out of the goodness of *our* hearts because *we* have been touched by *their* predicament. But protagonists of 'human rights' reject all this and insist that the poor and the oppressed have rights against us. The tone of this language is not warm and empathic but cold, peremptory, and demanding. It is not that we should be kind and generous towards the poor or the oppressed, it is that they possess rights and may make demands which we must acknowledge and strive to meet.

It is of course understandable that in the face of so much human suffering believers in human rights should be so vocal, but I am going to suggest two reasons to be sceptical. The first is that notions of human rights (unlike, say, charity or the relief of suffering) justify extensive, indeed in principle unlimited, interference in the societies (and the people) that are to be changed. In many ways this has already happened – there is now no aspect of African societies and Africans themselves, from their sexual habits to their dreams, that does not come under the sustained, often disapproving, gaze of Western agencies. The second, perhaps paradoxically, is that while the ideals of equality and human rights sound as though they require respect for others, in fact that respect is very partial. Where people are breaching 'human rights' we can be very aggressive indeed towards them, knowing that we are in the right and they are in the wrong. So in the rest of this chapter I am going to show how Western agencies have increasingly taken it upon themselves to change Africa, from the outside as it were, and the kinds of difficulty and mixed results that this has had in Africa itself. To get a handle on all this I will look first at the ways in which outsiders have tried to achieve development and then show how their disappointment with the results of those efforts has prompted firstly, close attention to African states, and secondly, closer attention to African societies.

The idea of development

The idea of development did not take its modern form until
after the Second World War and influenced colonial practice as
well as the process of decolonisation. Part of that process was a
tacit bargain with two parts. The first involved an historically
unprecedented commitment by one group of states to make
large-scale transfers of resources to another group of states. The
second involved the creation of a new set of official international
agencies (funded by states) some of which, notably the World
Bank, would have 'development' as their central concern. These
changes were supported by a large number of NGOs (non-
governmental organisations) concerned with both development
and lobbying for development. This bargain was understood in
a context of sovereignty. Both the new African leaders and
Western states agreed on the necessity and urgency of economic
growth and social change. The nationalist leaders promised to
make good on the promise of sovereignty by pursuing this goal
and Western states and development agencies promised to assist
them. There were tensions in this bargain that did not become
obvious until later. Implicitly the legitimacy and sovereignty of
African states was now permanently linked to their pursuit of
development. Should they fail in that pursuit, legitimacy and
sovereignty might come to seem an obstacle not a solution. A
second tension was that, even though development agencies
concerned themselves with only a narrow range of issues, they
were convinced they knew what was best for African countries.
In the event that development agencies started to broaden their
concerns, they would feel justified in pursuing much more
interventionist development policies.

Initially however all this remained in the future. For a long
time foreign aid was simply handed over to governments more
or less to do with as they chose. These aid flows have been and
are on a massive scale. The International Monetary Fund (IMF)

estimates that between 1960 and 2005 about US$650 billion in aid has been provided to sub-Saharan African countries by the Organisation for Economic Co-operation and Development (OECD) Development Assistance Committee (DAC) countries. This is the official aid from major Western donors and excludes non-DAC donors, such as China, India, and some of the Gulf states. The return on this huge flow of resources has been consistently disappointing, but what brought about the changes in the way it was delivered was the debt crisis, and the more general economic crisis, which overtook most African states during the 1970s and 1980s. Coincidental with shifts in economic policies in the West (symbolised by the advent of President Reagan in the United States and Mrs Thatcher in Britain), this crisis prompted a major rethinking of development theory and development policy among the big Western donors, and especially in the IMF and World Bank. The result was a shift away from the view that in underdeveloped countries the state was an essential instrument of development, to the view that the market mechanism was the 'magic bullet' that would secure progress. This reorientation of economic thinking then found expression in the policy of 'structural adjustment lending', essentially the idea that in exchange for economic support countries would adjust their economic policies in the direction demanded by the donors. But even this lending, initially at least, while certainly more intrusive than previous practices, remained broadly within the constraints of sovereignty, that is to say it was agreed between independent states and international organisations.

But structural adjustment lending contained the basic idea of 'conditionality' and this idea could be developed and extended in ways which, it was hoped, would get round some of the disappointments with aid. One idea was to dispense aid differently, hoping that new methods would produce better effects. So Western donors started to channel much more of their aid through NGOs. NGOs themselves eagerly backed this trend as it vastly increased their access to resources. Whereas before they had been rather dependent on small contributions from large numbers of individuals, now they could go after big money contracts offered by states and international organisations. They argued vigorously that they were better placed to implement development policies in Africa, partly because they had better access to 'the people' and partly because, not being mired in corruption and local politics, they were more effective than African states. Their voice was heard. By 1992 about US$8 billion was being channelled through development NGOs, about a quarter of the total. In 2000 the UN High Commission for Refugees budget, for example, was US$1 billion, most of which went to NGOs. NGOs have become Big Business.

Another way to change the delivery of aid was to develop the practice of 'conditionality'. What happened here was an increasing linking of aid resources to specific purposes and with specific conditions attached. Essentially, the goals of aid got more precisely defined and the linkages between the goals and the aid more precisely correlated. The IMF and the World Bank moved on from very general policy goals, such as privatisation of state assets or manipulations of the exchange rate, to much more detailed interference in the management of African economies. So for example these organisations might tell African countries that they should emphasise primary education and place much less emphasis on university education; or that they should introduce 'user fees' for education or health care; or that they should privatise their water supply. Another way was to require African countries to commit to large-scale public policy targets, usually involving the reduction of poverty. These are often rather rhetorical commitments to social welfare in the form of deadlines or targets, of which the best known are the Millennium Development Goals, which are commitments to end extreme poverty, achieve universal primary education, and reduce child mortality, among others (eight in all by 2015). African countries have not been slow to latch on to this latest fashion. Tanzania has a Vision 2025, so does Sierra Leone. Ghana has a Vision 2020. All of these make the same rather extravagant promises but offer little idea of how they are to be achieved.

The most dramatic way of extending the idea of conditionality yet devised is to require that African countries adopt specific types of economic management. In a number of African countries the international financial institutions have pressed African governments to contract out parts of their economic management structures, often their customs and excise service. But the most ambitious attempt to put in place such changes so far has been in Chad. The discovery of oil in that country necessitated a 1000 km pipeline to bring the oil to Cameroon. This was the largest single private investment in sub-Saharan Africa and could not have taken place without World Bank backing, both in terms of supporting the project as part of development, and investment of the Bank's own funds. The World Bank helped finance the Chad government's participation in the scheme on the strict condition that resources were invested in development sectors such as public works, education, health, and agriculture. To ensure this condition was met it set up an elaborate series of institutional constraints on the Chad government, which included channelling a portion of the revenues into a special account, placing limits on non-priority spending, and setting up a Future Generations Fund to receive 10% of all revenues. These allocations were to be overseen by a number of committees which included non-Chadians.

There can be no doubt that immense effort and ingenuity, both financial and human, has gone into 'development'. All the scares of a few years ago that aid to Africa was 'drying up' have proved to be wrong, indeed some governments (including the United Kingdom's) are increasing their aid even in a difficult global economic climate. There is little reason to doubt the genuine moral concern that animates this effort, though it is sometimes marred (as is any human activity) by bad faith. But we can ask two kinds of question about it. The first concerns its effects or its success: are some kinds of aid better than others? Does aid always have good effects? Does it sometimes have unforeseen effects? The second concerns its justifications: is it desirable? Should it be given at all? Are the reasons clear and compelling? It is not always easy to keep these two sets of questions apart, but it is important to get the best answers we can because all too often, aid is assumed to be, without question, a 'good thing'. To see why these questions should be asked let us glance briefly at Nigeria, Africa's largest, and one of the world's biggest, oil producers. Since the discovery of oil in the late colonial period the country has benefited to the tune of US$300–400 billion (estimates vary greatly). Nigeria is not, then, in any conventional sense 'poor'. But the mass of the people of Nigeria are. It is one of the thirty poorest countries in the world. Life expectancy is around forty-seven, possibly no better than late colonial times. We can also note that the Nigerian Institute of Management suggests that the country's leaders have since independence stolen an estimated US$480 billion from the national income. Is it clear beyond doubt that the outside world should be subsidising a country of such enormous wealth?

Many people who have reflected on this question have argued that there are a number of reasons to be sceptical about the value of aid. Much aid to Africa has been somewhat misconceived and unhelpful. As the Mozambique tractor example showed, the continent is littered with the debris of failed aid programmes, often because not enough is known about local circumstances and issues. So even if aid and donors are virtuous it is not obvious that aid has good effects. But are they so virtuous? The problem here is that giving and generosity are such powerful virtues that those who give take on an almost saint-like aura, and this is certainly an image of themselves that NGOs like to encourage. But development and aid have now become very big business indeed and are heavily influenced by Western governments and the international agencies they control. Many of the large aid agencies are now extremely dependent on official funding and have to meet the criteria of funding bodies. As elsewhere this leads to competition for contracts, a proliferation of projects aimed at donors (whose preferences can change) rather than the needs of poor people, and excessive rigidity in applying 'the rules'.

But let us assume that aid is well chosen and targeted and that the people involved in it are highly motivated by ethical standards and goals, which, more often than not, they are. There are still good reasons to wonder whether aid is a good thing. Many African governments have become hugely dependent on aid resources. For many of them ODA (aid) is still the largest source of capital inflows. Why might this be a bad thing? Because many African states can rely on fairly predictable flows of resources from outside the country they have not needed to rely on domestic taxation to fund public expenditure. When people pay taxes to governments they start to ask questions and make demands of that government. Many African states are considerably relieved from this pressure and have therefore been able to avoid the necessity of developing systems of personal taxation. There is a second effect of such large volumes of aid and this applies as much to African societies as to their governments. Many observers agree that very high levels of aid induce a kind of dependency complex amongst those in receipt of that aid. This effect is by no means limited to governments but affects private business and social organisations within Africa. This is not a particularly controversial point – after all the World Bank itself says that aid may have negative effects, 'by weakening political accountability, encouraging rent seeking and corruption, fomenting conflict over control of aid resources, and alleviating pressures to reform inefficient policies and institutions'.

Perhaps the most problematic aspect of aid, however, is not merely its paternalism but its condescension; its constant, if never actually stated, assumption not only that the donor knows best but that the receiver is a kind of empty vessel waiting to accept whatever bounty is showered on him. Let us return to Chad to see the force of this point. The oil started to flow in 2003. There was considerable domestic political tension in Chad in the first half of 2004 and the government could not for a time even pay its own soldiers. In 2005 it announced its intention to change the Revenue Management Law, breaching many of the restraints and allowing the government to spend more oil revenue money on non-developmental goals. The World Bank retaliated by suspending all further loans and freezing the oil revenues. President Deby now took advantage of both the regional political situation, threatening to expel Sudanese refugees, and the global oil situation, threatening to cut all production. Under pressure from the USA and France the World Bank negotiated an agreement that gave the Chad government much greater access to the oil revenue. In fact the World Bank effectively gave up. Deby now moved against the oil companies, Petronas and Chevron, implying they might lose their access to the oil fields. They paid up. By 2007 the Chad government had effectively removed all restrictions on the exploitation of its oil wealth. In 2008 Chad repaid its debt to the World Bank, whose involvement was effectively ended. Much of the discussion of this case has been about how 'we' could do it better. But should 'we' be doing it all? Perhaps assuming 'they' will do as they are told, or that 'we' should be telling 'them' what to do, is the problem.

Changing states?

Many people will angrily reject such scepticism. For them the Chad case exactly makes the point that to limit engagement with Africa to narrow questions of (economic) development is not enough. In this view the problem is that the aid and development agenda has always tended to hang onto the assumption that at some point African states would start to function as developmental agencies. But as the prospects for development in Africa came to seem more and more forlorn this possibility seemed less and less plausible. African states had proved incapable of effecting development, worse, had squandered many of the advantages they possessed. A large number of them were mired in conflict and political instability which they seemed increasingly unable to resolve or even control. Of course, such worries were expressed about other parts of the world (the Middle East, Central Asia) but they seemed particularly salient in Africa. They might have remained just worries but for the combination of a number of factors in the 1990s. While there remained much sympathy for Africa in general (as shown for example by attitudes to the Nigerian civil war or the Ethiopian famine), attitudes towards the African political class became increasingly hostile, as it was widely held to be responsible for conflict and instability. This was partly of course because, with the end of the Cold War, Western politicians no longer felt they had to defend African political elites. Indeed suddenly Western politicians were tumbling over themselves to pronounce on the importance of democracy in Africa. Even President Mitterand of France, not a country previously noted for its promotion of democracy, joined in the chorus, lecturing Francophone states that democracy was now the order of the day. But not only that. With the virtual end of South African apartheid in 1989 it became increasingly difficult to argue that this was the only African issue in which the outside world should take an interest, and so increasingly difficult to divert attention away from situations elsewhere in black Africa.

All these changes produced a much more intense focus on the African state and a much more openly critical account of its failings. A veritable torrent of disapproving terms for African states began to appear – 'failed' states, 'phantom' states, 'mirage' states, 'anaemic' states, 'vampire' states, 'aborted' states, even 'shanty' states. Combined with already widely held notions such as 'humanitarian intervention' and 'human rights' they formed a very potent brew. Clearly everything pointed to doing something rather dramatic about these states, but what exactly? One very serious difficulty immediately presented itself, namely that, like it or not, these were sovereign states with their own governments over which no outsider could (legitimately) exercise any control. The beginnings of a possible answer were, however, available, drawing on the experience of aid and development: the notion of conditionality. Surely if many of these states were not 'proper' states questions of sovereignty could take a back seat and conditionalities could be extended to the political realm. Just such arguments started to appear almost as soon as the Cold War ended. A flurry of statements from the Commonwealth, the European Union, the United Nations, and others appeared to the effect that African states must now change. But how exactly was this rather vague imperative to be cashed out? Once states themselves become an object of outside scrutiny and pressure three areas of activity suggested themselves. One is the institutions of the state, its structures and practices, in short its ways of doing things. A second is the political class or elite which in almost all societies is a very small section of the population, and in virtually all African societies, a minute proportion of the population. Again almost everywhere this elite consists of two rather distinct groups, politicians and officials. Finally, and most ambitiously, there is the political system as a whole, and the relation of that system to the wider society. All of these spaces in African politics have now become the target of intense outside pressure for change.

In the area of institutions the jargon word is 'governance', and the fact that until recently it was a rather archaic word in English tells us quite a lot about it. The World Bank in particular was looking for a word that encompassed the state but did not sound too political, and governance was a perfect fit. At first it was rather narrowly focused on the development aspects of state institutions but latterly, as so often the case with words in politics, it has come to take on a much wider range of meanings, including political legitimacy, accountability and transparency, and effective administration. What the notion of governance suggests is that, without effective institutions to make and enforce rules, especially those relating to property rights, there is not likely to be much 'development'. This was part of a general shift in ideas which began to acknowledge that, in Africa at least, 'the market' could not work miracles on its own but needed to be supported by a 'developmental' state. Once this idea caught on resources began to shift in this direction. In 2001 lending for public sector reform accounted for 14.5% of total Bank lending, up from 3.7% in 1997. There has also been a higher priority given to governance issues in terms of the organisation of the Bank. In a major reorganisation in 1997 a 'Public Sector Group' was created to focus the Bank's work on governance issues such as anti-corruption, civil service reform, legal reform, and decentralisation. This led to the creation of a World Bank strategy for improving governance in its borrower countries. It is quite a complex strategy, because in some ways it is designed to restrain states from doing certain things but in other ways it is designed to enhance their power.

But what did this all this mean in practice? An African country which has attracted much governance activity is Ghana. One aspect of this is the limiting of the scope of state action, so a prominent part of these programmes is privatisation and reducing the size of government. Nearly 200 government-owned or controlled agencies, ranging from the Ghana University Press and the National Theatre to the Ghana Tourist Board, have been privatised. The stated aim of the project is to create 'an efficient public sector'. A second aim is accountability and transparency. There is specific provision for putting 'private sector' business people on the boards of public organisations. In a recent Public Financial Management Project there is funding to improve the participation of civil society and other 'stakeholders' in the area of economic management. The project also supports capacity building activities for the media (training journalists and so on) so that 'it can effectively play its watchdog role vis-à-vis the fiscal and economic activities of the government'. The Bank is also engaged in attempting to clarify and codify the role of the state. According to the Bank, the state in Ghana suffers from a lack of clarity about the mandates of its agencies and their relationships with one another, and a lack of rules governing the use of human and financial resources. The project supports a programme designed to 'remove duplications and overlaps, develop new missions and roles, and realign functions' within the state. It will also attempt to introduce 'performance-based management principles' for some public services. Another project supports the implementation of a new institutional framework for Ghana's revenue-raising agencies. The final component of state reform is that targeted at making the state better able to govern its population. For example, a project in the late 1990s was focused around the development of a 'Tax Identification Number' system for all taxpayers. Along with the introduction of computerised tax records, this will enable the state to collect information and monitor the compliance of taxpayers.

Such measures are all very well but they have at least two drawbacks. The first is that they have to be accepted by governments and elites, the very people who are increasingly regarded as the problem not the solution. And secondly, such measures produce some new problems because like many aid projects they are tied to resources. There is always the danger, and at least the suspicion, that the aid tied to governance projects will be taken and then nothing much done, and to be fair, it is quite clear in many cases that this has happened. At this point we move onto much more controversial terrain which would have been unthinkable until quite recently. How might we change, even get rid of, incumbent rulers or political elites? What kinds of pressure can be brought to bear to ensure that the people actually running African governments listen to and take seriously, the messages of development and governance? This is sometimes called the problem of reform coalitions, that is, how to create among African elites a more receptive attitude to the message coming from Western states and international institutions. There are two ways of doing this. The first links up with developments we have already looked at in the context of humanitarian intervention and human rights. The International Criminal Court can indict public officials anywhere in the world for certain kinds of (international) crime. Although this is supposedly only for extreme cases it has encouraged the pursuit of other litigation across borders which would have been inconceivable even a few years ago. Even in circumstances where Western states have not wanted to override a country's sovereignty they can target politicians with certain calibrated pressures which, even if they do not drive them from office, nonetheless signal disapproval. These measures have included such things as asset freezing, travel bans, and more recently the funding of anti-corruption trials within countries or encouraging the bringing of anti-corruption cases against African leaders to Western courts.

But even these kinds of approach have their limitations. They are limited to threatening, cajoling, and nudging local political elites who have many cards in their hands, including a much better understanding of local political forces (this is what the Chad case shows). African politicians may, for example, quite happily use Western money to pursue corruption trials, or 'war crimes' but only of their political opponents, while their political friends remain strangely immune from prosecution. A more radical approach, then, towards reforming the African states might be changing ruling elites. This is a momentous step – once we take it we are talking about nothing less than the wholesale democratisation of African societies. We have come a long way from the details of economic policy or even the structure of government bureaucracies. We now contemplate changing whole political structures from the outside. How can this to be done? The magic word here is, of course, elections. Elections hold open the promise of tapping into local political forces and encouraging them to bring about change. Western agencies have made loud demands for multi-party elections in Africa, with dramatic effects. Recall that almost everywhere the form of the one-party state was adopted and that before 1991 not a single African government had changed hands as a result of an election. In 1991 that changed. Benin, Cape Verde, and Zambia all held multi-party elections in which ruling parties lost office and accepted the result. Since then elections have become the norm in Africa, and although there is the odd exception (Swaziland) and there have been an increasing number of military coups lately, virtually nowhere has the one-party state form returned.

Multi-party democracy in Africa is a relatively new development and its results, insofar as they are currently discernible, are more mixed than many observers like to admit. Pessimists tend to stress that, although Africans were fed up with the wretched performance of their governments, and there was much protest against them, it is not clear that this protest in itself was a demand for multi-party democracy. In one of the few countries which made serious enquiries about popular views, Tanzania, a commission of enquiry found that a large majority were against the idea of multi-party democracy. The Tanzanian government went ahead and introduced it anyway. In this view African elites were responding to both sticks and carrots. Western demands for 'democracy' were quite tough and there was little to be gained by defying them. But Western states were also prepared to put up money as well. Mozambique held its first multi-party elections in 1994. They cost something like US$65 million, of which Mozambique paid perhaps US$5 million. These were rather special circumstances (the end of a bitter conflict) but they give some idea of the sums involved. The 2007 elections in Nigeria, one of the world's big ten oil producers, were subsidised by the EU to the tune of millions of euros. Elections are popular with Western donors because they are big, newsworthy 'events', because they are not open-ended, and because they play well to sceptical audiences back home. With widespread elections in Africa has come a whole industry of electoral observation, teams of observers ensuring that elections are 'free and fair'. Those observations also suggest reasons to be sceptical, that in many cases (recently Nigeria and Kenya) elections are shamelessly rigged, and they have failed to dislodge the elites who are so often thought to be the barriers to progress. In short, many African political elites have learned to use to their own advantage something that initially seemed so threatening, often by sharpening religious and ethnic conflict to get voters to the polls.

Optimists quite rightly point to other significant trends. Some countries (Ghana, Mozambique) have now had four or five elections and it seems increasingly unlikely that they will return to more authoritarian politics. In a number of countries electorates have prevented politicans (e.g. Chiluba in Zambia and Muluzi in Malawi) changing constitutions so that they could have a third term in office. African parliaments have increasingly begun to bestir themselves and, if not challenge governments, at least ask probing questions about policy and financial matters.

There is no question that the newspaper and electronic media are much freer than they were and African people are able to be more informed about what their governments are up to. The reaction to the more sceptical perspective is to suggest not that Africa needs less aid towards democracy but rather that it needs more and deeper political change. In part this involves going beyond the narrow parameters of elections to the wider political process. It is not enough, so the argument goes, simply to hold elections, what is needed is a more democratic political system. This would require much greater engagement with political processes, for example, support for political parties and pressure groups, for changes in the legal framework within which parties operate, and for reforms in the management of print and electronic media. All of these features of African political systems now attract intense Western interest. But all these measures, though they are dramatic extensions of the involvement of Western agencies in the politics of African states, remain within the political realm. Other voices are increasingly calling for change that goes beyond the political realm. What, after all, is politics, but the mobilisation of social energies? Perhaps it is not merely politics than needs changing but the very fabric of African society itself.

Changing societies?

We have arrived at a rather bleak account of African politics which suggests that it is the inadequacies of African elites, particularly political elites, which are at the heart of the problems of the continent, an assessment which seems to imply increasingly fine-tuned and intrusive efforts to reform political, and especially state institutions. Despite the gloominess of this assessment, many people find it quite congenial or at least more congenial than other possibilities. Unlike the nineteenth century which was quite comfortable with ideas of a hierarchy of civilisations, we live in an age when beliefs in human equality are widespread and deep-seated. This generates a dilemma. If things are not as they should be whose fault is it? It cannot be 'the people' for they are (must be) like us. It must therefore be their leaders. This response has further advantages because it suggests action. If only we could deal with these bad men in some way then 'the people' would flourish. But as soon as one looks at states one finds that they cannot be understood without examining their relationship to the wider society. Almost without thinking this is where many activists and policy makers have now found themselves.

Changes in African states seem to demand changes in African societies, but how is this to be done? How can you change whole societies? There are roughly two kinds of strategy currently in play, one concerning civil society and another concerning human rights. The term 'civil society' is a useful bit of social science jargon that describes the field of social activity between the purely private on the one hand, that is individuals and families, and the state on the other hand. So roughly speaking it means any kind of organised social activity which is not overtly political (so it excludes things like political parties). The theoretical details are not so important for us here, all we need to bear in mind is that, in the view of its proponents at least, civil society makes possible the representation of diverse social interests, balances the power of the state by providing an arena of criticism and debate, and encourages participation among citizens. Why is this notion so attractive in relation to Africa? Because it seems to provide an answer to the problems of the limitations on influencing the African state from outside, and even on democratic elections within Africa.

The key idea here for Africa reformers is the notion of 'accountability', that is making sure that governments actually listen to the views of the people. But as we have noted even elections will not have this effect if there are not organised social forces within the society for the state to be accountable to. Whatever changes are urged on African states the fact of the matter is that, unless local political forces hold African states to those changes, they may not happen. So civil society strategies concentrate on supporting those segments of African society that seem to be, or are likely to be, supportive of the reforms being pressed on African states. So as international organisations, Western states and Western NGOs became more and more disenchanted with African states they began to look around for other avenues by means of which to influence African societies, and began to funnel very large sums into African NGOs (sometimes called civil society organisations). In the ten years between 1984 and 1994, the British government increased its funding to NGOs by almost 400%. By 2000 NGOs in Africa managed nearly US$3.5 billion in external aid, compared to less than US$1 billion in 1990, roughly 20% of total aid to the continent. Africans were not slow to see where the money was going and, particularly in a period of drastic retrenchment of public employment, many saw NGOs as their salvation. Not surprisingly there was an explosion of NGOs in African countries. In 1980 Ghana had eighty registered NGOs; by 2001 it had 1300. Tanzania had twenty-five NGOs in 1986; fourteen years later there were more than 10,000. Uganda had 200 registered NGOs in 1986; by 2007 there were 7000.

Many in the West wanted to believe that all this was evidence of the development of civil society. While it is true that in some cases NGO aid has resulted in well-organised projects that have rooted themselves in local circumstances and realities, it is also the case that much of this aid consisted of what are often known in Africa as 'briefcase NGOs', that is new opportunities to tap into aid money. As one Uganda NGO director put it in an interview, 'Look, I am not going to be shy about this — this is in the first place a business. We first think of our own survival, secondly about other people's survival'.[1] In pursuit of such resources projects of all kinds were proposed to catch the eye of donors, and more sceptical observers have tended to suggest that this has had two negative effects. The first is that far from enhancing African capacity it has rather induced extreme dependency. Many African NGOs tailor their requests to what donors want to hear and those that master the currently fashionable jargon or concerns (environment, gender equality, poverty reduction) get the lion's share of the resources. Those able to do this are, of course, overwhelmingly concentrated in the modern, particularly urban, sector of African societies. While Africa is urbanising fast it is still very rural, and rural people have very little say in such organisations. One expert suggests that in Tanzania (which is a huge aid receiver):

> the donor desire to fund civil society institutions has actually undermined the formation of civil society in pastoralist communities. The bureaucratic logic of international development requires that money be given to Tanzanian NGOs, regardless of their capability of bringing about democratic change. In many cases, NGO leaders become gatekeepers between Western donors and the communities that they wish to assist. More energy is spent in accommodating donor ideas and meeting reporting requirements than in empowering local people. Communities become commodities of an international NGO industry, rather than active participants in Tanzanian civil society.[2]

As this assessment suggests, far from empowering the poor and the weak civil society aid may strengthen the powerful and those well connected with the state.

The second issue that needs comment in relation to civil society strategies concerns a very simple dilemma, though Western commentators are remarkably reluctant to face it. There is a kind of conceptual arrogance built into the very idea of civil society and related strategies, namely that no kind of society existed before. But Africa has always had its own forms of social organisation, even if many in the West have been reluctant to acknowledge them. These include more 'traditional' forms like age sets, secret societies, clans, or lineage groups as well as more 'modern' forms like home town associations and ethnic associations; and of course, after extensive contact with the West and various processes of social change, they now include more easily recognisable (to us) bodies like trade unions, church groups, pressure groups, and so on. In a descriptive sense we can regard all these as 'civil society'. The trouble is that many in the West, and often those who are most committed to changing Africa, find many such organisations objectionable on various grounds, or rather insist that they work according to Western principles. These principles include gender equality, social equality generally, and internal democracy. 'Social justice', a prominent Western activist tells us, 'demands the eradication of all forms of discrimination, whether on grounds of race, creed, tribe or sex'.[3] Notice the tone of this entirely typical remark – other people's practices are to be 'eradicated'. If we define civil society in these terms then much actual African civil society disappears. On the other hand many of these associations and organisations appear to work quite effectively at delivering services, Muslim welfare associations for example. To put it simply: what we like is not what works and what works we don't like.

It is in part the response to this dilemma that opens the space for the relevance of the notion of human rights. Here we have to do a little more unpacking because the proponents of human rights often make things seem obvious when they are not. If we look at human rights advocacy it invariably focuses on cases of (what appear to be to us) gratuitous human suffering. So for example, Amnesty International waged a major campaign in northern Nigeria over Shari'ah (Islamic law) penalties for adultery. But this is in part tactical, just as animal rights activists proclaim the rights of seals or donkeys rather than those of spiders or cockroaches. There is much more to the notion of human rights than this. Consider the International Convention on the Rights of the Child, one of the most widely ratified documents. This document tells us that a child is a human being between birth and eighteen years (clause 1). This is not obvious. Many people, certainly in Africa but not just there, think that foetuses are human beings, and many people in Africa think that people younger than eighteen are not children and, in some cultures, that people much older than eighteen are still children. Human rights, then, are not an obvious, universal set of values. They are a particular set of values, predominant in the Western world, presented as universal. Indeed, even in the West, as the issue of abortion shows, there is not complete consensus. And we might note that the Convention on the Rights of the Child did not fall from the sky but was the result of hard political bargaining. So the attraction of this idea must be more than that it identifies and condemns suffering. Beyond the concern with suffering it offers a template of life which applies to everyone, irrespective of their culture or indeed their opinions. It authorises, then, condemnation of and legitimates interference in, the practices of others. The parallels with Christianity in an earlier historical period, indeed in Africa up to the end of the nineteenth century, are remarkable and illuminating. People might be ignorant of the word of God but, having heard it, if they did not accept it, they were wicked and could be chastised. Human rights is a secular faith.

The best example of this dynamic is probably the largest campaign about human rights in Africa, and concerns what is variously known as female circumcision or (by its opponents) female genital mutilation. An examination of this issue casts a sharp light both on African societies that practise it and on Western reactions to it. Quite a large number of African societies, often Islamic but by no means exclusively so, practise some form of modification of the female genitalia which can vary between very minor incisions to removal of significant parts of the pudenda. Such practices are invariably part of an understanding of what is the appropriate transition from girlhood to womanhood, connected to ideas of honour and sexual propriety, and thus marriageability and social acceptance. A massive campaign has been waged against it, not merely by women's organisations and human rights groups but by international organisations and Western states. This campaign likes to present itself as concerned with the poor conditions and threats to health that such practices involve, but on closer examination this proves to be a red herring, as these issues could be resolved by improved medical conditions. After all many operations, including cosmetic ones popular and acceptable in the West, can be dangerous. The objection then is much more fundamental and concerns gender and sex, and especially sees female circumcision in African cultures as an oppression of women. It has been condemned by many organisations as, variously, an extreme form of discrimination against women, a violation of the rights of the child, and a violation of the rights to health, security, and physical integrity of the person. This campaign did not pick up speed until the 1990s and has taken a variety of forms, including that of increasing pressure on African states to criminalise such practices and attaching conditionalities as a form of pressure. Even the IMF and the World Bank have added their weight to these demands. Out of some twenty-eight countries in Africa where female circumcision is practised, sixteen have now passed laws forbidding it.

But a great deal of research shows that female circumcision is carried out by women and that, if anything, African men are more likely to be opposed to the practice or more easily persuaded to abandon it. How, then, to explain this? The campaigners then argue that this is a form of 'false consciousness', that such women are sunk in tradition and backwardness from which they must be liberated by emancipated Western women (and men). The tone of much of this campaign has been and is astonishingly aggressive. Phrases such as 'unspeakable atrocities', 'torture', 'pathology' are regularly bandied about and demands for 'eradication' are quite normal and assume that African parents are malign and wish to harm their children. Some African voices have been raised against this sort of vocabulary, protesting against the malice that for example the term 'mutilation' ascribes to parents. We can add to these considerations the point that those who have looked at the evidence have found that the health risks of many (though not all) kinds of circumcision have been greatly exaggerated or based on very inadequate studies. As Dr Carla Obermeyer has suggested, 'the current state of the evidence does not allow hasty pronouncements about all the harmful effects attributed to circumcision.'[4] So we need to look elsewhere for a fuller explanation of this campaign. We can see that it is rooted in shifts in attitudes towards sex and gender relations in the Western world (attitudes which we may well think are appropriate to our own societies).

These are of course sensitive issues, about which people can feel very strongly, but it is precisely such issues that need the most careful consideration. There are many other customs, concerning for example widowhood practices or the raising of children, that we might consider reprehensible but that form integral parts of other people's cultures. What is not clear is that our attitudes should be imposed on others who do not share them and indeed have very different attitudes to questions of sex, gender, relations between the sexes, and family life more generally. What this example shows, I suggest, is not merely that attempts to change other people's societies are fraught with difficulty, especially because they discount the possibility that those other people may have views and agendas of their own different from ours, but also that our attempts to interfere often stem as much from our own certainties and cultural arrogance as any concern for others. Both, I suggest, should make us very sceptical about all such interventions.

Another kind of change?

In 2005 Ethiopia held elections. During the election campaign the ruling party repressed opposition parties, shot demonstrators on the street and used all the power at its disposal to win, which it duly did. International observers attended these elections and their judgements on them were fairly scathing, they were certainly not deemed to be free and fair. In 2008 there were more elections in Ethiopia, this time for local office. The ruling party continued to use the full weight of the state machine against its opponents and was again 'successful', winning 99% of the seats. The difference this time was there were no international observers, no outside agencies to comment on the elections. What had changed? Almost certainly what had changed was the assessment of the major powers, and particularly the United States, of the politics of the region and Ethiopia's role within it. That assessment was shaped by a relatively new development in world politics, the so-called 'war on terror', a rather misleading label for the reaction of the United States to the attacks on New York in September 2001. In Africa that response has included a much more hostile attitude towards Islamist political movements, as in Ethiopia's neighbour, Somalia. Ethiopia has projected itself as a loyal US ally in the region and was effectively given the green light in July 2006 to invade Somalia to secure the defeat there of Islamic political organisations. It has also facilitated the so-called 'rendition' and interrogation of suspects wanted by US intelligence agencies. The United States is now Ethiopia's largest bilateral donor. This case, and other similar situations, suggest to many people that much of what I have been discussing so far in this chapter is rather trivial, even misleading, in that it obscures behind a screen of pretty words about democracy, development, and human rights the real motives of outside actors in Africa, which turn out to be wealth and power. How true is this?

The argument comes in two forms, one more historical and one more contemporary. The historical one we have touched on already in this book and I do not need to say a great deal about it here. It is true that in addition to the 'civilising' attitude towards Africa there has been a 'business' attitude. It was present during the slave trade period and the decades before the 'scramble', and to some extent between the Second World War and the end of the Cold War. This attitude took Africa as it was and looked for opportunities to make money and exercise influence. I do not want to downplay the significance of this at all, indeed I would go further and suggest that in some ways this was a healthy attitude towards Africa. But I have argued that it has not usually been the predominant attitude towards the continent. This brings us to the second, more contemporary, version of the argument, which suggests that, even if I am right about the historical past, recent changes are making for a decisive shift in outside stances towards Africa, much more governed by calculations of wealth and power. There are three factors that are usually pointed to, and although they are interlinked in various ways they all need some comment. The first is the greatly increased activity of China throughout the African continent; the second developments in oil markets and their political implications; and the third the so-called 'war on terror'.

Of the enhanced role of China in Africa there can be no doubt. Although China had a record of activity in Africa before the recent developments that was largely shaped by the context of the Cold War, but more particularly the Sino-Soviet conflict (when the Chinese slogan was an anti-Soviet one 'against hegemonism'). The more recent phase post-dates the incidents around Tiananmen Square in April and May 1989, when the

Chinese government ruthlessly suppressed domestic opposition, as a result of which China found itself widely condemned and isolated internationally. African states showed some sympathy for China's position and, partly as a response, China embarked on a much more active diplomacy aimed at the underdeveloped world, and especially the African countries. Its slogan now was 'China is the largest underdeveloped country in the world', stressing its solidarity with others. A second issue in this diplomacy is the campaign to persuade the world that Taiwan is a part of China and not an independent state. Only four African states now recognise Taiwan. The other obvious factor is the rapid expansion of the Chinese economy, now the third largest in the world after the United States and Japan. The astonishingly rapid rate of growth of the Chinese economy has meant a rapid rise in its consumption of fossil fuels. It is projected that its oil consumption will more than double by 2025. China is the second largest oil importer after the USA and imports 30% of its oil from Africa. Its largest presence is in the Sudan, where it owns 40% of the largest oil-producing company in the country, but it has been acquiring stakes in Nigeria and Angola, Africa's two largest producers. China's economic relations with Africa are, however, by no means limited to oil or even to trade, it has also been investing in mining and a variety of infrastrcture projects such as dams, roads, and railways. The evidence seems very strong that these are long-term calculations and that China means to have a considerable presence in Africa.

Despite this diversity it is the connection between China and the world's oil production that has excited the most interest. The bulk of the world's oil reserves remain in the Middle East (a notoriously volatile region), so China is not the only oil consumer looking to Africa. Both China and the United States have small, declining levels of domestic oil production. Both are also seeking to diversify their sources of supply. There are many advantages to African oil. African countries are heavily dependent on the export of raw materials and therefore cannot afford to leave their oil in the ground. It is often of high quality and therefore needs less refining, and is often located offshore (Angola, Nigeria, Equatorial Guinea) and so is less likely to be affected by political disruption. Finally, Africa is the least well geologically mapped region of the earth and if there are to be major finds they may well be on the continent, as recent prospecting and discoveries in Tanzania, Uganda, and Ghana suggest. For all these reasons, then, there has been intense interest and involvement in the oil sector in Africa.

There are also links between these two factors, China and oil, and the third to be discussed here, 'terrorism'. Terrorism is a notoriously slippery term and is more often used to discredit political movements than explain them. That said, two things are indisputable. Some groups in the Muslim world have been prepared to resort to armed struggle of various kinds either in pursuit of resistence against Western domination of the Muslim world or to establish more properly 'Islamic' regimes (and what this might mean is of course controversial, even among Muslims). And powerful forces in the West, notably but by no means only elements within the United States government, have argued that terrorism is a, or even the, major danger in the world today, and justifies a 'war on terror'. Even if some of the policies pursued by the Bush administration are modified or abandoned these attitudes remain influential in certain circles. What are the implications of all this for Africa? The most obvious point is that large parts of Africa are Muslim and therefore not entirely removed from developments in the Muslim heartlands. It is certainly the case that religion is becoming a more salient feature of African politics generally, and Islamic radicalism may grow in Africa where it can draw on African traditions and history, for example the jihads (holy wars) in pre-colonial Nigeria. The demands for sharia law in northern Nigeria in recent years are only the most obvious example of this. There may well be a harsh response to this on the part of both African governments and the West. Despite the US taking the lead in the so-called 'war on terror' governments around the world have not been slow to see the political advantage in identifying their domestic opponents as 'terrorists' (as China itself does in Tibet and Sinkiang), hoping to legitimate whatever treatment may be meted out to them.

Peering into the future we can suggest two more points. We should of course bear in mind that things might change – China may experience more internal upheavals, oil prices fall as well as rise, new technologies become available, the West may shift its position on 'terror' – all of which makes prediction hazardous. But there is a dynamic here which is having a major effect on Africa's international environment. It seems likely that the combination of the global distribution of oil, political militancy in at least parts of the Muslim world, continued if not increased Western hostility to any challenges to its hegemony, and the determination of China to become a global power, as well as the emergence of 'middle rank powers' such as India, Brazil, possibly Indonesia, will all ensure a continued interest in the world's last great mineral treasure house, the African continent. It is inevitable also that even if outside powers claim to be avoiding interference in Africa, given the unstable nature of much of the continent, they will in fact be dragged into greater involvement. This is clearly the case with China already. As Chinese economic activity in Africa grows it will comes under greater scrutiny and be exposed to more criticism, as recent protests about working conditions in Zambia have shown. And despite its claims of non-interference China has already become involved in Sudan, providing troops as part of a UN mission, and exerting pressure on the Khartoum government to listen to the UN on Darfur.

The other trend we can identify, which also looks set to continue, is that the combined effect of these factors will be to give African states more room for manoeuvre, both economic and political, than they have had since the end of the Cold War. The advantages for African oil producers are self-evident. They can avoid the burden of debt, which hugely reduces the leverage held over them by international financial institutions, and they can exploit rivalries between different oil companies and their parent governments. Even the non-oil producers have more choices, for development aid, trade, and political support, with China active in Africa. The very presence of China on the continent may strengthen those voices in the West that suggest (at the moment very quietly) that we must deal with Africa as it is, not as we would like it to be. This of course would be to abandon the twenty-five years or so of lecturing Africa and attempting to change its behaviour from outside to which many agencies have been committed. So the least we can say is that there is an increasing tension between an improving agenda (promoted by Western civil society and its domestic African allies and more or less supported by Western states and the international organisations they control) and a more 'realist' agenda based on calculations of advantage and interest. The crucial question is, of course, whether Africa can exploit these opportunities to achieve some of its own objectives.

By way of conclusion

I began this book stressing that it was going to be hard-headed look at realities, and that is what I have tried to provide. It is not the task of academics to tell people what to think, but it is part of their task to try and be clear about the effects that certain ways of thinking have and to suggest other possible ways of thinking about things. So by way of a conclusion I am going to draw out what in my view are some of the most important themes about Africa's place in the world today, and then discuss some of the ways in which we think about them. Four points about contemporary Africa seem to me to be so plain that they must remain in the forefront of our reflections. The first is that, relatively speaking, life in Africa has been, and is, hard for human populations, though this is of course compounded by the absence, until recently, of technologies that could moderate that environment. Such difficulties look set to continue. Even if some well-known hazards, for example certain tropical diseases, are, or can be got under control, new threats have taken their place such as HIV/AIDS, and there are almost certainly others on the horizon, notably the effects of global warming. It is not environmental reductionism to suggest that African experience has been profoundly moulded socially and culturally by its material and geographic context.

The second is that although the African continent has been, over long periods of time, heavily influenced by the outside world, it is the internal dynamics of African societies that remain predominant. There is room of course for much argument about the specifics of certain kinds of influence but, propaganda aside, it is clear that while those outside influences have sometimes been destructive (the slave trade), they have also been constructive (modern science and technology) and decidedly ambiguous (Christianity and Islam). What counts is what Africans themselves have made (and will make) of these forces. My third point is that partly, but by no means only, because of these factors, African societies are extremely resilient and have a capacity to absorb and recover from adversity which is remarkable. This is not to proclaim a kind of soggy romanticism about Africa but to make a point about a capacity for social organisation that many peoples in the West have long lost.

Of course many readers may find these remarks somewhat exasperating: well yes, they might say, let us suppose all this is true, but what difference does it make? What is to be done about children dying of curable diseases, or people who lose everything to floods or locusts or violent political conflict? It is certainly the case that being hard-headed need not mean being hard-hearted, but we shouldn't be soft-headed either. So the tendency to instant emotional reaction needs to be tempered by thinking. This leads me to my fourth point. The one incontrovertible imperative, it seems to me, is that if African societies are to solve, or at least alleviate, the many problems they face they must make the transition from being predominantly low productivity agricultural societies to more diversified ones which generate more wealth and especially employment. In a word they must become more productive. This might all seem blindingly obvious, but I suggest that the voices supposedly speaking loudest on Africa's behalf, both in Africa itself and in the West, have rather lost sight of it. Indeed, as I suggested in the introduction to this book, much contemporary discussion and debate, both academic and popular, is suffused with a kind of political correctness which has had very damaging effects. It is at least a two-way trade. On the African side there is a widespread blame and dependency culture. Every problem and difficulty is the fault of the West and everything is to be corrected by demanding vast 'reparations' for the crimes of the past. But the absurdities of all this should be readily apparent. Are the descendants of African slaves entitled to reparations against their historic African owners? Are the descendants of Europeans captured as slaves by North African pirates also entitled to reparations? How does this nonsense get off the ground? Because it flatters an equally unhealthy combination on the side of the West, this time of guilt and arrogance. The current fashion for apologising for political events in the past says something about the emotional mood of the times but it will not build a single factory or prevent a single African child dying of malaria. But underneath this rather cheap and tawdry guilt is an equally repulsive cultural arrogance which does little to disguise the unthinking assumption that our standards are better then everyone else's and we are entitled to impose them on others. Because African countries are poor and weak the 'development agenda' becomes bloated with every Western concern (gender, environment, rights, the disabled) to which Africans are expected to show immediate deference and compliance.

If we can release ourselves from this suffocating political correctness two things may become possible. We can attain a certain clarity and modesty about our aspirations and objectives. Nowhere in history have societies achieved industrialisation, democracy, gender equality, and environmental sustainability all at the same time, and it is absurd to expect Africans to do so. So for example if, as I have argued, the elites who assumed power in the newly independent states, or at least many of them, did in fact take seriously the task of hastening the progress of their countries, albeit in almost entirely Western terms, the possibility arises that this was a much more difficult task than they, or indeed anyone else had anticipated, for reasons to do with the nature of those societies. This in turn requires that we take seriously the idea that societies can be very different in their organisation and culture and these differences have real consequences for the way people behave. This is an idea that many people find difficult to accept, especially in relation to Africa, because it seems to hark back to old, and discredited, notions about inferiority and irrationality. But all it does in fact is require is for us to try and make sense of and describe in as level-headed a way as possible how societies actually work, and to set aside any sense of moral superiority (which does not of course require us to set aside notions of moral difference).

The acknowledgement of historical and sociological realities need not lead to counsels of despair or inaction. It may make possible the application of imagination to Africa untrammelled by outside agendas and fashions. There have been strong tendencies to lump all the 'bads' together – witchcraft *and* chief-taincy *and* corruption *and* gender inequality *and* authoritarian government and so on – all of which should be swept away, ideally as soon as possible. But this is nonsense. Bits of culture are only 'good' or 'bad' in contexts. Strong group loyalties may be bad in a context of violent conflict between ethnic groups, but they may be wonderful in a context of environmental hazards or the absence of a welfare state. Even things like corruption are not 'bad' in some definitional sense. Great Britain in the eighteenth century, when it began its rise to great power, was, by modern standards, hugely corrupt. The fact is that Africans have cultures just as everyone else does, and that is where they must start. What have we got and what can we do with it? Within the context of the imperative to become more productive, if chieftaincy works, use it; if gender equality is desirable, which social practices should be encouraged to change first, and which might be left alone? And if ethnic identity is good for certain things, draw on it or adapt it, don't try to suppress it. If, on the other hand, people have agreed to abandon certain bits of culture they no longer think are productive or suit their way of life (and this is happening all over Africa) then so be it; but let that be because they have decided to, not because the West or its 'experts' tells them to.

Notes

Introduction

1 http://news.bbc.co.uk/1/hi/8356357.stm (accessed 2 March 2010)

Chapter 1

1 P.J. Hotez and A. Kamath, 'Neglected Tropical Diseases in Sub-Saharan Africa: Review of Their Prevalence, Distribution, and Disease Burden', *PLoS Neglected Tropical Diseases* 3(8), 2009, e412

2 Hari Eswaran, Russell Almaraz, Paul Reich, and Pandi Zdruli, 'Soil Quality and Soil Productivity in Africa', United States Department of Agriculture, Natural Resources Conservation Service, http://soils.usda.gov/use/worldsoils/papers/africa3.html (accessed 2 March 2010)

3 B. Davidson, *The Black Man's Burden: Africa and the Curse of the Nation State*, New York, Random House, 1992, p.216

4 J. Iliffe, *Africans: The History of a Continent*, Cambridge, Cambridge University Press, 1995, p.68

5 J. Lonsdale, 'States and Social Processes in Africa: A Historiographical Survey', *African Studies Review*, 24(2/3), 1981, p.139

6 Adrian Hastings, *The Construction of Nationhood: Ethnicity, Religion and Nationalism*, Cambridge, Cambridge University Press, 1997, p.155

7 Quoted in Gareth Austin, '"Developmental" Divergences and Continuities between Colonial and Pre-Colonial Regimes: The Case Of Asante, Ghana, 1701–1957', unpublished paper, p.11

8 C. Wrigley, *Kingship and State: The Buganda Dynasty*, Cambridge, Cambridge University Press, 1996, p.6

Chapter 2

1 Quoted in N. Ferguson, *Empire*, London, Allen Lane, 2003, p.269

2 H. Temperly, *The Times Literary Supplement*, 25 June 1999

3 S. Gunn, 'The Ministry, the middle class, and the "civilizing mission" in Manchester, 1850–1880', *Social History*, 21(1), 1996, pp.22–36, p.36

4 R. Tombs, *France 1814–1914*, London, Longmans, 1995, p.203

5 Chief Commissioner Fuller quoted in G. Austin,'"Developmental" Divergences and Continuities between Colonial and Pre-Colonial Regimes: The Case Of Asante, Ghana, 1701–1957', unpublished paper, p.12

6 Alexander Moradi, 'Towards an Objective Account of Nutrition and Health in Colonial Kenya: A Study of Stature in African Army Recruits and Civilians, 1880–1980', Centre for the Study of African Economies, Working paper 2008–04, p.23

7 T.C. McCaskie, 'Cultural Encounters: Britain and Africa in the Nineteenth Century', in A. Porter (ed.), *The Oxford History of the British Empire, vol.111 The Nineteenth Century*, Oxford, Oxford University Press, 1999, p.688

8 T. Mboya, *Freedom and After*, London, Andre Deutsch, 1963, p.61

9 Abubakar Tafawa Balewa quoted in J. Herbst, *States and Power in Africa: Comparative Lessons in Authority and Control*, Princeton, NJ, Princeton University Press, 2000 p.112

Chapter 3

1 These quotations can be found in T. Young (ed.), *Readings in African Politics*, Oxford, James Currey, 2003, p.1

2 J. Iliffe, *A Modern History of Tanganikya*, Cambridge, Cambridge University Press, 1979, p.550

3 P. Geschiere (ed.), *Readings in Modernity in Africa*, Oxford, James Currey, 2008, p.1

4 T. Mkandawire, 'African Intellectuals and Nationalism', in T. Mkandawire (ed.), *African Intellectuals Rethinking Politics, Language, Gender and Development*, Dakar, Codesria, 2005, p.24

5 James C. Scott, *Seeing Like a State. How certain schemes to improve the human condition have failed*, New Haven, CT, Yale University Press, 1998, p.241

6 Frantz Fanon, *The Wretched of the Earth*, London, MacGibbon & Kee, 1965, p.139

7 The *Guardian*, 19 May 1979

8 http://news.bbc.co.uk/onthisday/hi/dates/stories/february/3/news id_2714000/2714525.stm (accessed 4 March 2010)

Chapter 4

1 E. Luttwak, 'Give War a Chance', *Foreign Affairs*, 78(4), 1999, pp.36–44

2 M. Albright quoted in G. Dempsey with R. Fontaine, *Fool's Errand: America's Recent Encounters with Nation Building*, Washington, Cato Institute, 2001 p.25

3 See www.iccwatch.org (accessed 4 March 2010)

Chapter 5

1 Julie Hearn, 'African NGOs: The New Compradors?', *Development and Change*, 38(6), 2007, pp.1095–110, p.1103

2 Jim Igoe, 'Scaling up Civil Society: Donor Money, NGOs and the Pastoralist Land Rights Movement in Tanzania', *Development and Change*, 34(5), 2003, pp.863–85, p.881

3 J. Clark, *Democratizing Development: the role of voluntary organizations*, London, Earthscan Publications, 1991, p.30

4 Carla M. Obermeyer, 'The Health Consequences of Female

Circumcision: Science, Advocacy, and Standards of Evidence', *Medical Anthropology Quarterly* 17, 2003, pp.394–412, p.408. For further discussion see C. Obermeyer, 'The Consequences of FC for health and sexuality: an update on the evidence', *Culture, Heath and Society* 7(5), 2005, pp.443–61

Further reading

Chapter 1

There are a number of good general histories. I have leaned heavily on John Iliffe, *Africans: The History of a Continent*, Cambridge, Cambridge University Press, 2007, which has a useful emphasis on population. For a rather different approach try Phillip Curtin, S. Feierman, L. Thompson, and J. Vansina, *African History From Earliest Times to Independence*, Harlow, Longmans, 1975. For Buganda see C. Wrigley, *Kingship and State: The Buganda Dynasty*, Cambridge, Cambridge University Press, 1996, especially the last chapter which is well written and commendably frank about trends in African history writing. There are huge debates about the Asante kingdom. The classic texts are I. Wilks, *Asante in the C19: The Structure and Evolution of a Political Order*, Cambridge, Cambridge University Press, 1975, which perhaps tends to present a rather idealised account, and T.C. MacCaskie, *State and Society in Pre-Colonial Asante*, Cambridge, Cambridge University Press, 1995. These are long, demanding books but are full of interest.

Chapter 2

F. McLynn, *Hearts of Darkness: The European Explorations of Africa*, London, Pimlico, 1993 is a lively account of pre-conquest European contact with Africa which brings out the range of attitudes. It is fashionable to condemn books like N. Ferguson, *Empire: How Britain made the Modern World*, London, Allen Lane,

2003, but it is well written, excellently illustrated and raises important questions. More hostile to colonialism and very long, but also very readable, is T. Packenham, *The Scramble for Africa: White man's conquest of the dark continent from 1876–1912*, New York, Perennial, 2003. For colonialism at its very worst, look at Adam Hochschild, *King Leopold's Ghost: A Story of Greed, Terror, and Heroism in Colonial Africa*, Boston, MA, Houghton Mifflin, 1998. Stanley, who later in life broke with Leopold, may have been unfairly treated by historians. See T. Jeal, *Stanley: The Impossible Life of Africa's Greatest Explorer*, London, Faber and Faber, 2007. For a different time and a different angle, see J. Lewis, *Empire State Building: War and Welfare in Kenya 1925–1952*, Oxford, James Currey, 2000.

Chapter 3

A clear survey of the political history of independence is M. Meredith, *The State of Africa*, London, Free Press, 2006. More scholarly but well focused and well written is P. Nugent, *Africa since Independence: A Comparative History*, London, Palgrave, 2004, which also covers the issues of development. J. Herbst, *States and Power in Africa: Comparative Lessons in Authority and Control*, Princeton, NJ, Princeton University Press, 2000, is useful on the difficulties African states have faced in consolidating their power and authority.

Chapter 4

M. Berdal and G. Malone (eds), *Greed and Grievance: Economic Agendas in Civil Wars*, Boulder, CO, Lynne Rienner, 2000 covers much of the debate about 'new wars'. C. Clapham (ed.), *African Guerillas*, Oxford, James Currey, 1998 has many interesting case studies of particular movements. On intervention, Mats Berdal and Spyros Economides (eds), *United Nations Interventionism, 1991–2004*, Cambridge, Cambridge University Press, 2007 has chapters on Somalia, Sierra Leone, and Rwanda. Most Western academics are in favour of humanitarian intervention. M. Mamdani, *Saviors and Survivors: Darfur, Politics and the War on Terror*, London, Verso, 2009 raises many questions about the issue of intervention as well as providing a detailed account of the struggles in Darfur, Sudan. For more detail on Somalia see M. Brons, *Society, Security, Sovereignty and the State in Somalia: from statelessness to statelessness?*, Utrecht, International Books, 2001; for Sierra Leone see L. Gberie, *A Dirty War in Africa: The RUF and the Destruction of Sierra Leone*, Bloomington, Indiana University Press, 2005; for the Congo see Thomas Turner, *The Congo Wars: Conflict, Myth & Reality*, New York, Zed Books, 2007. T. Murithi, *The African Union*, Aldershot, Ashgate, 2005 is a good summary.

Chapter 5

For a very vigorous African critique of aid see D. Moyo, *Dead aid: why aid is not working and how there is a better way for Africa*, London, Penguin, 2010. This book has sparked much controversy. A good place to start following it is the reply by one of the West's leading advocates of aid, Jeffrey Sachs, at www.huffingtonpost.com/jeffrey-sachs/moyos-confused-attack on_b_208222.html (accessed 4 March 2010). For a critical African view of NGOs see M. Amutabi, *The NGO Factor in Africa: The Case of Arrested Development in Kenya*, New York, Routledge, 2006. For a recent survey of the issues see R.A. Dibie, *NGOs and Sustainable Development in sub-Saharan Africa*, Lanham, MD, Lexington Books, 2008. On the World Bank see G. Harrison, *The World Bank and Africa: The Construction of*

Governance States, London, Routledge, 2004 and the path-breaking analysis in D. Williams, *The World Bank and Social Transformation in International Politics*, London, Routledge, 2008. On human rights issues see A. An-Na'im (ed.), *Cultural Transformation and Human Rights in Africa*, London, Zed Books, 2002. For a sample of views on circumcision see O. Nnaemeka, *Female Circumcision and the Politics of Knowledge*, Westport, CT, Praeger, 2005. On China see I. Taylor, *China and Africa: Engagement and Compromise*, London, Routledge, 2006 for a good recent survey. On oil Ricardo Soares de Oliveira, *Oil and Politics in the Gulf of Guinea*, London, Hurst, 2007 is an excellent study.

Index

A Beginner's Guide to
Fair Trade

Packed with inspiring ways to make a difference, author and activist Jacqueline DeCarlo explains why Fair Trade means so much more than just bananas, coffee, and chocolate.

"Articulates the history and future

978-1-85168-521-9 | £9.99

of our movement, outlining the challenges in front of us and the opportunities for consumers to make a tremendous impact by choosing fair trade." **Carmen K. Iezzi**, Executive Director, Fair Trade Federation

"From coffee farmers to consumers, ceramics to certification, DeCarlo brings to life the history and depth of the Fair Trade movement." **Rob Everts**, co-Executive Director, Equal Exchange

"Fantastic. For anyone that has ever wondered about what 'fair trade' means, this Beginner's Guide tells you everything you ever wanted to know and more." **Alexandra Spieldoch**, Director, Trade and Global Governance Program, Institute for Agriculture and Trade Policy

JACQUELINE DECARLO is Fair Trade Program Advisor of Catholic Relief Services, and former Director of the Fair Trade Resource Network.

Browse further titles at
www.oneworld-publications.com

Beginners
GUIDES

A Beginner's Guide to Democracy

David Beetham offers new insights into the role of the citizen and how large corporations affect democracy as well as contemplating the future of democracy in the developed and developing worlds.

978-1-85168-363-5
£9.99/ $14.95

"Beetham's book should stimulate anyone, beginner or expert, who is interested in the survival and renewal of democracy in the era of globalization." **Peter Singer** – Author of *The President Of Good And Evil: Taking George Bush Seriously*

"A strong and shrewd mixture of analysis and polemic…If more was not to come, I would call this the author's crowning achievement." **Sir Bernard Crick** – Advisor on citizenship to the UK government

DAVID BEETHAM is Professor Emeritus of Politics at the University of Leeds, a Fellow of the Human Rights Centre at the University of Essex, and Associate Director of the UK Democratic Audit.

Browse further titles at
www.oneworld-publications.com

A Beginner's Guide to The Middle East

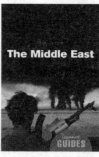

9781851686759
£9.99/ $14.95

This compact book by the University of Oxford's leading expert is stuffed with historical background, real-life examples, profiles of key figures from Nasser to Gadaffi, and even popular jokes from the area. *The Middle East: A Beginner's Guide* will captivate tourists, students, and the interested general reader alike.

"Masterly. A comprehensive and succinct overview." **Hugh Pope** – Former Middle East Correspondent for *Reuters, Wall Street Journal,* and the *Independent*

"The best book on the modern Middle East. Perfect not only for students but for any reader. It is balanced, authoritative and easy to follow. A perfect introduction to this troubled region." **Christopher Catherwood** – Author of *A Brief History of the Middle East*

PHILIP ROBINS is Reader in Middle East Politics at the University of Oxford. He is the author of *A History of Jordan* and has previously worked as a journalist for the BBC and the *Guardian*.

Browse further titles at
www.oneworld-publications.com

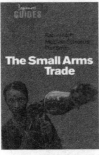

A Beginner's Guide to The United Nations

9781851687527
£9.99/ $14.95

In this well-written and informative guide, Norrie MacQueen provides a clear introduction to UN institutions, remit, personalities, and role in the modern world. Defending it from common criticisms of bureaucratic paralysis and bias towards the developed world, MacQueen argues that its limitations are due to the complex web of national interests that it seeks to reconcile.

"Balanced, reliable and engaging." **Robert Faulkner**, Senior Lecturer in International Relations, London School of Economics

"Coherent, concise and wide ranging. This guide does exactly what is required." **Mark Imber**, Senior Lecturer in International Relations, University of St Andrews

NORRIE MACQUEEN is Senior Lecturer in International Relations at the University of Dundee. He is author of several books on the United Nations and a world expert on UN Peacekeeping

Browse further titles at
www.oneworld-publications.com

A Beginner's Guide to Crimes Against Humanity

978-1-85168-601-8
£9.99/ $14.95

Using examples ranging from
the genocides in Darfur and
Rwanda to the use of torture
in the 'war on terror,' Jones
explores the progress made in
toughening international law,
and the stumbling blocks which
prevent full compliance. Coherent and revealing, this book is
essential for anyone interested in
the well-being of humanity and
its future.

"Jones has written a much-needed conceptual overview
and call to action which will wake people up to the
worst of which humanity is capable." **Charli Carpenter**
– Assistant Professor, Department of Political Science,
University of Massachusetts Amherst

"A remarkable book that is immediately accessible for the
novice in the field, or students, and yet also engages with
its topic in intellectually interesting ways for the more
seasoned reader." **James Gow** – Professor of International
Peace and Security, King's College London

ADAM JONES, Ph.D., is Associate Professor of Political
Science at the University of British Columbia Okanagan,
Canada.

Browse further titles at
www.oneworld-publications.com